45 DAYS

WALKING THE BIBBULMUN TRACK

Also by Diane Eklund-Āboliņš

Novels:
The Space in Between
Room Nineteen

(after 2015)
The Waiting Room
An Ambiguous Tragedy
Kaleidoscope

Poetry:
On the Circle
Glänsande vitt på blått

45 DAYS

WALKING THE BIBBULMUN TRACK

Diane Eklund-Āboliņš

Published by AoE Publishing 2015

Copyright © Diane Eklund-Āboliņš
All rights reserved

The moral right of the author has been asserted

This work is copyright. Apart from any use as permitted under *Copyright Act 1968*, no part may be reproduced, copied, scanned, stored in a retrieval system, recorded, or transmitted, in any form or by any means, without prior written permission of the publisher.

First published in Australia in 2015 by
AoE Publishing
Sydney, Australia
Revised edition 2023

ISBN: 978-0-9873473-4-3

Typeset in Times New Roman
Cover design: Annette Abolins
Photography: Diane & Andris
Printed and bound by LSI

Included maps are approximations
and are not to scale.

As well as minor changes to the text and images, this revision includes some information regarding Track updates since the 2015 publication.

Dedication

The book is dedicated to all those people who made the Bibbulmun Track a reality and to all those who continue to make it a possibility.

Introduction

Why would anyone in their right mind *choose* to walk more than one thousand kilometres through blistering heat, freezing cold and torrential rain; along seemingly never-ending, isolated, sandy beaches; over hills and boulders, many of them masquerading as mountains; through dense bush and forests or across open, windswept plains? Why would anyone want to remove themselves from all the warm and cosy creature comforts we normally take so completely for granted?

For most people the answer is perfectly clear: any such person would have to be at least slightly mad. Yet, at the same time as the majority of people might be relegating such a proposition to some imaginary folder marked C*razy*, there would certainly be a few who would be able to see past the thin veneer of supposed madness to the challenge. These few people would most likely understand just what that challenge was offering: the promise of solitude and the escape from civilization.

The experience, not just of being alone but of being completely at one with the landscape, is very special, and, while some people might be happy to rush through areas of singular beauty in well-equipped vehicles, constantly in search of the next photo opportunity or simply because they want to be able to tick off one more thing as completed, the landscape can only be properly understood when we are able to relate to it physically. It is necessary to be able to feel sand and rocks and prickly bushes against our skin, to smell leaves and grasses and to sense the numbing reality of cold creek water against our bare legs. We cannot properly understand the landscape until we are able to feel some kind of affinity with it, and when there is only us and the landscape this sense of closeness becomes not only self-evident but also very special.

Challenges are important. Back in the day, when we had to chase and subdue our dinner, survival itself was the major challenge, but a trip to the local supermarket in the twenty-first century is definitely not the same kind of experience, not even by a long stretch of the imagination. Many might attempt to call the supermarket excursion a challenge of sorts, but it is not quite the type of challenge I had in mind.

When dinners are minus legs, efficiently frozen and wrapped in plastic, and when, outside the gym, physical exertion is kept to a minimum we often need to find, or even create, our own challenges. If we do not challenge ourselves, mentally, physically and even emotionally, there is often a danger of stagnation. By surpassing the limitations and the need for conformity imposed upon us both by society and our own innate fear of being different we are usually able to find ourselves. Accepting and then meeting a challenge is an amazing feeling: it is, I feel, the closest we will ever come to knowing who we really are.

The ten years that have passed since we walked the Bibbulmun Track have not changed the experience – that is not possible – and the story of our Walk is exactly the same now as it was when it actually happened. No matter how much we may sometimes want to, we cannot change the past.

It had always been my intention to write about the Walk, and whenever I could during our six weeks on the Track, I took notes, filling the pages of a couple of exercise books that gradually became the more and more worse for wear as the Walk progressed. Then, when I finally had the time and space to start pulling everything together, I began to wonder if anyone would be interested, and I shelved both the notes and the idea.

Other things squeezed in until I had completely forgotten on what shelf I had placed everything, and then, purely by chance, I read *Tracks* by Robyn Davidson (an account of her 3,000-kilometre journey from Alice Springs to the Atlantic Ocean). I really enjoyed the book and decided that perhaps there might actually be people out there who would be interested in reading about a 1,000-kilometre walk from Albany to Perth.

This is definitely not a *How to Walk the Bibbulmun Track* information book – there are already some excellent books for anyone wanting helpful, practical information about the Track[1] – it is simply an account of

---

[1] We used a two-volume, pocket-sized *A Guide to the Bibbulmun Track*, published by CALM. The edition I have is the 1st Edition

our Walk. Our experiences on the Track will not be exactly the same as other people's experiences on the Track, in the same way as other people's experiences will, with all likelihood, not even begin to parallel ours. It is more than possible that others would have responded very differently to many of the situations and experiences we encountered along the Track, but then this is not their story; it is ours. What I have written may inadvertently give some tips and information, but that was never the primary aim of the book.

Over the following pages, you will read about how the Walk came about and, more importantly, what it was like walking one thousand kilometres from Albany, in the Great Southern region of Western Australia, to the outskirts of Perth, the state capital, about four hundred kilometres to the north-west as the crow flies.

To *think* about walking one thousand kilometres is daunting; to do so is a challenge on many different levels. Even though there were times when I definitely questioned our sanity, the indescribable sensation of being so very much at one with nature while being completely removed from the noise and stress of everyday living, together with the sense of achievement when we finally accomplished what we had set out to do, put everything into perspective. It was one of the most difficult Walks I have ever done, but it was also the most rewarding and, in so many different ways, the most satisfying.

> from 1998; however, the two-volume edition was updated in 2014 (and again in 2018) and now comprises eight books. Unlike the original publication, these books do not contain any maps and must be used in conjunction with the Bibbulmun Track Maps. Check the Bibbulmun Track website for more information: https://www.bibbulmuntrack.org.au

❂❂❂❂❂❂

In February 2001, I flew to Tasmania with my husband, Andris, and did the Overland Track – a five-day Walk through the extremely rugged and beautiful scenery in the north-west corner of that state. Unlike many of the other Walks we have undertaken, it is a very popular Walk, which means that the campsites are usually filled to capacity with tents, people and cooking smells.

I do not particularly like walking together with lots of other people, and I cannot see myself fitting into the traditionally accepted image of a bushwalking group. It is not that I do not like other people – quite the opposite – but walking as part of a group would in all probability negate what for me are the two most important aspects of long-distance walking: the isolation and the relative silence. Fortunately, when we did the Overland Track, the various groups of walkers that met up at the campsites in the evenings conveniently managed to disappear along the Track during the day, and, for most of the time, Andris and I were actually walking in our own, very isolated, space.

It was at the campsite on the first evening of the Walk that we met up with Heather and Chris from Western Australia, and we continued to catch up with them for a short chat on most of the ensuing evenings. While we talked about the Track and things related to the Track, it was inevitable that the conversation would eventually move on to other Walks – both those we had done and those we still hoped to do. Heather mentioned that she and Chris had recently walked a small section of the Bibbulmun Track in Western Australia. Describing the long list of difficulties they had encountered while negotiating particularly daunting sand dunes, she shook her head and said that they had found it all far too demanding and that it was highly unlikely that they would do any more of the Track.

I had never before heard of the Bibbulmun Track, and I was trying to get my head around the strangeness of the word when Heather went on to say that the whole Walk measured just over one thousand kilometres. Immediately, my interest was sparked – a Walk measuring one thousand kilometres would *have* to be absolutely fantastic.

During the rest of 2001, the idea of doing the Bibbulmun Track remained very much in the background as there were too many other things demanding my attention. In May 2002, Andris and I did the Hume and Hovell Walk in south-west NSW – a 450-kilometre Walk between Yass and Albury – and then, as 2002 moved closer towards 2003, I finally began to think more seriously about the Bibbulmun Track.

In early 2003, I contacted the Bibbulmun Track Foundation in Perth and spoke with a lovely lady called Gwen, who sent me a lot of information about the Walk. Having taken this first step, I was already looking forward to what was ahead of us, and I was actually beginning to make a rough plan of the Walk in my head. Then, at the end of April, Andris suffered chest pains that necessitated a stay in hospital and a barrage of tests, and the idea of doing any kind of walk, least of all one that stretched over one thousand kilometres, suddenly became completely unimportant.

ӨӨӨӨӨӨ

By December 2004, I was becoming quite desperate to do another long Walk. For me, walking is a meditative exercise, a kind of anti-stress activity, and I regularly have an overwhelming need to get as far away as possible from the noise and the visual overload that are the unfortunate appendages of our present-day lifestyle. The occasional walk around the block is simply not sufficient.

Although Andris had not experienced further chest problems, he had felt unwell on a few occasions and was understandably hesitant about doing any serious walking. Because of safety concerns, I was not at all keen to do such a long Walk on my own (together with a definite propensity for getting lost, any semblance of bravery disintegrates after nightfall) and, no matter how I looked at it, I could see no way around the problem. Then, in January 2005, I happened to mention the Walk to my younger son, Jonathan. He was on the verge of finishing one job and moving on to something different, and he said that he would love to do the Walk with me.

The Walk was actually going to happen, and the certainty, while stimulating, was also somewhat daunting. I was excited, relieved and even terrified. I am sure that I briefly wondered about all the things that had to be planned and whether or not everything would come together in time. I know that there were several occasions when I was almost completely overcome by the enormity of the challenge on which we were about to embark: the reality was, at times, just a little terrifying. One of my diary entries, written when I was momentarily swayed by some people who felt that such a project was completely insane, shows that I was no longer quite sure that I was doing the right thing. But, in the very next entry, I wrote that it was important that I should believe in myself, and that is exactly what I ended up doing.

Based on Jonathan's window of availability and the possible weather patterns for the south-west corner of Australia, we decided to start sometime in mid-March. Allowing seven to eight weeks for the Walk, this meant that, all going well, we would probably be able to enjoy pleasant autumn weather for most, if not all, of the Walk.

I applied for time off from work, and in February, with not much more than a month remaining until we hoped to set off, I once again contacted Gwen at the Bibbulmun Track Foundation in Perth. This time I inundated her with questions: Did the Walk normally take eight weeks? What was the best way of replenishing supplies? What kind of weather could we expect in March, April and May? Should we walk north to south or south to north? Should the water at the campsites be filtered? Was there mobile phone coverage anywhere on the Track?

Gwen (no doubt slightly overwhelmed by all the questions) told me about their Trip Planning Service and gave me the contact details for Don, one of the Friends of the Bibbulmun Track. She assured me that Don would be happy to answer any questions I might have about the Walk. In the meantime, she told me that it probably made more sense, given the time of year we were planning to do the Walk, to walk south to north, that is to say from Albany to Perth. When I emailed her with the comment that walking from Albany to Perth made it feel as though we would be going uphill all the way, she got back to me, saying that I would be surprised at the number of people who had said exactly the same thing.

Whether or not Don was overwhelmed is difficult to say, but he was definitely extremely helpful; in fact, without his support and patience, I doubt that I would have been able to manage the large amount of planning that had to be done in such a short space of time.

Apart from giving us good advice about water (water should not be drunk from any of the streams or creeks without treating it first), supplies (limited supplies along the Track, but also the option of posting food parcels), mobile phone coverage (none to very poor) and a variety of other things, Don felt that eight weeks for the Walk was a good average. He said that a few people have actually managed it in thirty days, while others can take seventy days and even longer. He also pointed out that there is a lot of beach walking in the relatively flatter southern section, and that negotiating sand dunes and long stretches of beach with a full pack can be quite difficult, something with which we would later come to agree one hundred percent.

From Don we learnt that the Walk is divided into three sections – Albany to Northcliffe: mainly coastal landscape with some forests; Northcliffe to Balingup: big forests and valleys; Balingup to Kalamunda: hills and relatively small trees. He doubted that we would experience too much rain during March and April, and felt that a start in Albany should allow us to miss the high temperatures often associated with Perth even in the latter part of March.

Things were beginning to come together. On the calendar in the kitchen, I took a pen and drew a circle around the 19th March as the start date for our Walk, and I wrote long lists of things that had to be organized, things that were already organized, things I did not want to forget, things that I *must* not forget…

Then Andris said that he had decided that he would join us for a couple of weeks on the Track, even if he had no intention of walking every one of the one thousand kilometres. It was wonderful that he wanted to be part of the Walk, but, given the fact that he had been unwell, I was dubious. He assured me that it was something that he wanted to do and that he definitely felt that he could manage it. After a lot of discussion, it was decided that he would meet us in Walpole and that he would then walk with us as far as Balingup. According to my plan, this meant that Andris would arrive in Walpole on the evening of the 28th March, and that he would leave Balingup on the morning of the 16th April.

Things were becoming more and more real with every passing day.

ϴϴϴϴϴϴ

The Bibbulmun Track stretches for almost one thousand kilometres from Albany, on the south-west coast of

Western Australia, to Kalamunda, on the outskirts of Perth. As lengths given for the Track vary between 956, 963, 973, almost 1,000 and 1,003 kilometres – possibly dependent on track diversions or the state of the tape measure used – it is probably more correct to say that the Track covers a distance of somewhere between 956 and 1,003 kilometres.

On a map, the Track resembles an L, with the vertical running south from Kalamunda to Northcliffe, and the horizontal stretching from Northcliffe to Albany along the southern coastline.

The Walk is very varied: it crosses coastal headlands and beaches, runs through old-growth forests, plantation forests, dense bush and heath lands, and climbs up and down hills and across large expanses of granite.

There are around fifty campsites along the Track, all of which have a three-sided, timber shelter, a rainwater tank, a picnic table and a pit toilet. There are two or three different designs, which normally accommodate about ten people quite comfortably. Apart from the three sides and roof, which give much needed protection against the weather, the shelters are basically not more than a slightly raised timber floor on which the weary walker can roll out a sleeping mat and a sleeping bag.

The Track itself passes though a number of small towns or villages: Albany, Denmark, Peaceful Bay, Walpole, Northcliffe, Pemberton, Donnelly River Village, Balingup, Collie, Dwellingup and Kalamunda, all of which offer some kind of alternative accommodation, with showers and washing facilities, as well as somewhat varied opportunities to purchase supplies.

Not all walkers walk the whole Track end-to-end:

some walk it in sections over a period of years, with the aim of eventually covering the entire Track; others simply do an occasional day walk or weekend walk. For anyone interested in doing the Track – all of it or a small part of it – the very best source of information is the Bibbulmun website: https://www.bibbulmuntrack.org.au/

A number of black-and-white photos from the Walk have been included throughout the book; however, a larger selection of coloured images can be viewed online at: https://diane.eklund.abolins.net/45.html

Kariong to Perth

Thursday 17th March (St. Patrick's Day) was the day of our departure from Kariong, seventy kilometres north of Sydney. The weather, unfortunately, could hardly have been worse; it was not particularly cold – the temperature was around 20°C – but rain had been relentlessly pouring down from a grey and overcast sky since early morning. To make matters worse, the fan belt on Quentin (our 1981 Volvo station wagon) had broken the previous evening. Andris had immediately contacted the garage in Kariong regarding a new belt. The mechanic had been extremely sympathetic and promised to have the belt delivered by the following morning. The only problem was that he ordered the wrong one.

I have no way of knowing how the mechanic felt when he realized what he had done. It is more than possible that it did not faze him overly much, but no matter how he may have felt, he managed to pull all the necessary strings and have the right belt at the garage by late Thursday morning. As a result, Andris was able to have Quentin out of his sickbed and running on all four wheels by early afternoon, and we were able to discard our hastily thrown together emergency plan of catching a bus to the railway station.

As well as the weather being against us and the car not functioning, I had picked up some kind of virus that had been doing the rounds. In spite of swallowing a whole army of Zinc tablets, vitamin C, Echinacea, throat lollies, water and aspirin, in the hope that at least something would prove to be a miracle cure, I was still feeling awful, and I was beginning to suspect that the army had broken up into a number of small factions, and that they were also waging war against each other. While my body hankered after a prone position and several blankets, my mind was kept busy, checking through my many lists, searching for anything that was still not ticked off.

Jonathan arrived from Sydney around midday, fully aware that he would soon be back on the train doing the reverse journey. We had first considered meeting up at the airport, but being practical I knew that there was always the chance that one of us could miss a connection and not arrive in time; eventually, we agreed that it would probably be safer if we both started from Kariong. Also, there were many things that had to be shared between the two packs, and it was probably not ideal to be unpacking and repacking backpacks on the floor of the airport terminal.

Sometime in March, after all the arrangements for the Walk had been made, one of our daughters, who lived in Brisbane, said that she and her family would be dropping in for a few days before moving to Sweden for twelve months. As it turned out, they were to arrive the following Tuesday, by which time Jonathan and I would be well and truly on the Track. During our daughter's stay in Kariong, Andris was also expecting a short visit from one of our overseas friends. The timing of both visits was not the best, but there was not much to be done about it: as always, everyone was locked into pre-arranged schedules, and it was just a matter of going with the flow.

By four-thirty, with Quentin clutching his newly signed certificate of good health, we were ready to leave for the railway station; the rain had, however, not relented, and it was no easy matter to organize ourselves and our backpacks into the car while fending off the incessant deluge. We knew that the six-kilometre trip between Kariong and Gosford usually took about ten minutes, but none of us had given any thought to the fact that the weather had been playing havoc with the traffic. Already, as we turned out of Kariong on to the main road, there were long lines of wet cars, with steamy windows and rhythmically moving windscreen wipers, banked up as far as we could see. The frustration behind the blurry windows was unmistakable, a fitting complement to the many black clouds above us.

The estimated ten minutes had disappeared well before Kariong disappeared from the rear-view mirror, and we were all holding our breath and whispering silent prayers as the ten minutes were replaced by twenty and then, to our great consternation, by thirty. With the train to Sydney due to leave Gosford at ten minutes past five, I was seriously beginning to doubt that we would get to the railway station in time.

Arriving at the drop-off bay outside the station at five minutes past five, we had very little time to say goodbye to Andris, buy our tickets and scramble down two flights of stairs to the platform while fighting against the formidable tide of returning commuters. We fell on to the train with our packs in our arms, and had barely managed to seat ourselves before the automatic doors closed, and the train pulled out of the station.

The stressful journey to the station, together with the fact that the warring pills and virus were refusing to declare any kind of ceasefire, had not made me feel any better. Also, it was still pouring rain, and everything had that grey, waterlogged, miserable tinge to it that is usually the result of hours of constant rain. It was definitely not the most ideal start to what we hoped was going to be a wonderful experience. However, on the other hand, we had not missed the train (if we had, we would most certainly have missed our plane connection to Perth), so we decided that perhaps there was a small sliver of blue amid all the grey after all.

An hour and a half later, we reached Sydney Central Station and then took a suburban train to the Domestic Terminal.

The airport was decked out in shamrocks and signs wishing everyone a happy St. Patrick's Day. As I was responsible for choosing the check-in queue everything that consequently happened was probably partly my fault.

Usually the person at check-in greets the intending passenger with a smile; even if the smile can sometimes seem a little artificial, it is an indication that the person concerned is at least somewhat pleasantly disposed to the customer.

Our check-in person was not at all pleasantly disposed to anyone. She glared at us for a moment, without speaking, before demanding, "Destination?" When she failed to hear my answer, she repeated herself even more arrogantly. There were definitely no smiles here, which made me suspect that someone was having a much worse day than we had been having.

Although the lovely, smiling attendant at the check-in next to ours was placing two backpackers' packs (complete with rolled-up sleeping mats) into large plastic trays, *our* attendant sharply blurted out, '*Everything* has to be in the pack!'

It did not require a lot of intelligence to see that this was a physical impossibility, and I told her as much, leaving out the bit about the amount of intelligence required. However, *this* had nothing to do with physical possibilities or impossibilities: if the regulations require everything to be in the pack, then everything *must* be in the pack. I really did not have much to lose – it was unlikely that she could be more unpleasant than she had been already – so I drew her attention to the fact that the attendant at the next check-in had actually allowed two fellow travellers to leave their packs exactly as they were, with attachments. Icily she replied that she could not answer for anyone else, but the regulations stated quite clearly that luggage was not to be checked in with attachments. I am not sure if the other check-in attendant squirmed at this obvious criticism of her actions; I was too busy detaching all my attachments, which had been very carefully strapped to the pack in view of the impending plane trip.

The queue behind us grew longer and longer as I fumbled with all the straps, and eventually Jonathan had to come to my rescue. Then it was his turn, and though the tent pegs were safely secured in a pocket on the side of his pack, he was told that they would have to be removed. We stood there in front of the check-in counter, balancing an array of sleeping mats, tent accessories, tent pegs and other bits and pieces, while the attendant issued our boarding passes. There were a number of things I would have liked to have said, but I breathed in very deeply and said nothing.

However, if we now thought that the worst was over, we were deluded; what we had so far experienced was unfortunately only the beginning.

We made our way to the security check and thankfully offloaded all our assorted bits and pieces into a couple of the familiar, blue plastic trays. As the plastic trays moved along the roller bed and into the X-ray area, there was a small flurry of excitement as the middle-aged officer checking the screen saw the 'long, sharp sticks'.

"What are they?" he asked a much younger officer standing next to him, his voice taut with anxiety. The other man moved closer to the screen and almost immediately answered the question: "Tent pegs! Long and sharp! No way!"

I nervously explained what had happened at check-in, expecting any moment that we would be dragged to one side, escorted to a waiting police car and then driven to the closest gaol at high speed.

Fortunately, this did not happen, but it did not take me very long to reach the conclusion that Security is probably several steps up the hierarchical ladder and abides by a completely different set of regulations to those followed by check-in staff. According to Security's interpretation of the regulations, the 'sticks' were definitely a security hazard and would not be allowed in the cabin of the plane, not under any circumstances. They would have to be checked in.

Back to check-in strode Jonathan, the offending tent pegs in his hand, and our not-so-pleasant attendant, perhaps understanding that she had now been well and truly checkmated, labelled the package with the offending sticks and sent it off on the conveyor belt – a small lonely package on its own.

When Jonathan returned, minus sticks, he discovered that he was also minus his boarding pass, and he had no option but to make yet another trip back to the check-in attendant, to either find the boarding pass or, as it turned out, have a new one printed. I am quite sure that the attendant had, by this time, been forced to accept that not only had she lost the battle but she had also lost the war, and she was doubtlessly looking forward to knock-off time. According to Jonathan, she had even dropped the harsh façade and was almost bordering on being pleasant. Whether this was because she had completely given up, was on the verge of a nervous breakdown or was having second thoughts about her people skills is difficult to know.

As a result of all this excitement, we arrived at the gate with very little time to spare. It was already 7.40 pm, and the plane was due to board ten minutes later, thirty minutes before take-off.

We were told that the flight would take four hours and twenty-five minutes. With Western Australia two hours and thirty minutes behind Sydney, we calculated that we would land in Perth around ten-thirty; however, because of favourable flying conditions, we actually landed just after ten.

We collected our packs from the baggage carousel and were relieved to see that our tent pegs had survived the trip without getting lost, even though they did seem somewhat awed and overwhelmed by all the heavy luggage swirling around them. As we exited the airport, the warm evening air rushed at us, taking us slightly aback: it was still 25°C after a top of 30°C earlier in the day, and there was not a drop of rain anywhere. Arriving from a very rainy, cool east coast, the mild, dry weather was a pleasant welcome.

There were not a lot of people waiting for taxis, so we had no trouble finding one to take us to the Britannia Youth Hostel in Northbridge, an inner-city suburb of Perth. Our first impressions of Perth from the windows of the taxi were that it seemed fairly clean (but, of course, it was dark), that there did not seem to be much traffic (but it was late) and that the roads were very wide.

The youth hostel looked as though it had been part of the Perth landscape for quite some time, and from what we could see, it covered one whole block. Once inside the building, we were met by a rambling maze of stairways that spread out from the entrance and reception, and, after checking in and receiving the keys to our rooms, we followed one of the stairways to the second floor.

In my room, I made a few adjustments to my packing, and then went to bed. With the fan not working, it was very hot. Although I was quite tired and it was after midnight, it took a long while before I finally fell asleep.

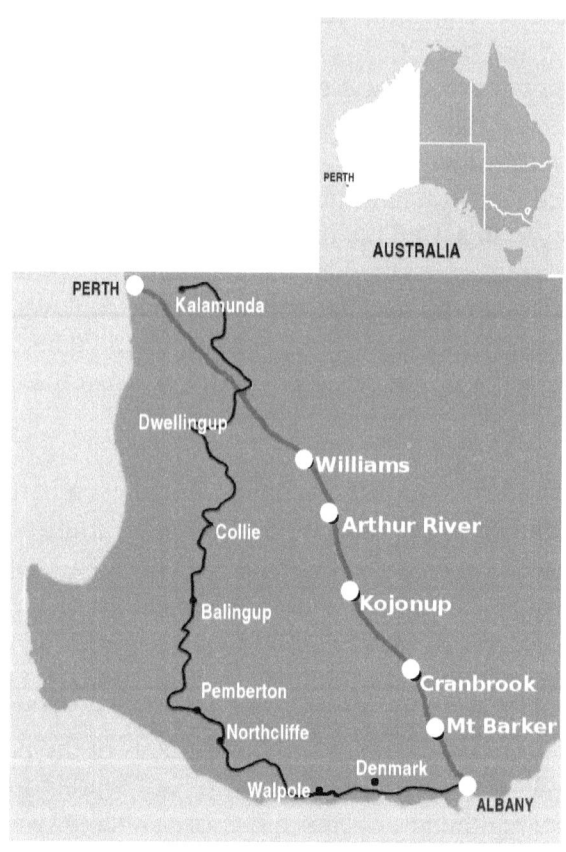

Albany Highway and the Bibbulmun Track

Perth to Albany

On the morning of Friday 18th March, I was up well before six. I had not slept at all well, and, although I had set the small two-dollar alarm clock bought expressly for the Walk, I woke long before it was due to ring.

While I was having a shower in the ladies' toilets at the far end of the corridor, I was startled by very loud, pounding music coming from an aerobics class in the brick building next door. Looking through the row of high windows above the washbasins, I could see many energetic lycra-clad people moving in time to the music. For obvious reasons, I found it all quite daunting – I was still feeling quite hung-over from the virus, and I was trying not to dwell too much on the fact that we would be setting out on our very long Walk in less than twenty-four hours.

After breakfast, we walked the short distance to the central station to catch a train to East Perth, the weight of the pack (eighteen kilos give or take) making itself unpleasantly obvious. I knew that Jonathan's pack was *well* over twenty kilos, so I focused on convincing myself that I really had nothing to complain about.

Our packs contained everything we needed on the Walk; unlike a suitcase lugged along on an overseas holiday or a two-week getaway, there was absolutely nothing in the pack that could not put up a good argument for its being there. Nothing was thrown in 'just in case'; 'just in case' was simply not an option.

Before I actually put everything in the pack, I made a long list of all the things I believed I would need, then I weighed everything (and I really do mean *everything* – I even weighed my toothbrush) and diligently listed the weights next to the objects on the list.

Then I began to remove things that had lost the chance to be included on the basis of their weight. After I packed everything into the pack, I tried it on for weight; when it felt too heavy, keeping in mind that two to four litres of water still had to be added, I pulled everything out of the pack and started all over again.

Perth's central station, like most central stations, is large, open and very airy. It was even quite busy when we were there but nowhere near as busy as the central station in Sydney.

From the station we caught a train the few stations to East Perth and then walked to the bus terminal; we did not have long to wait before the bus to Albany arrived just before nine. Thankfully we stowed our packs in the luggage compartment underneath and then climbed on to the bus. We discovered that our allotted seats were not next to each other but that we both had a window seat, which we decided had to be an advantage on a six-hour, 400-kilometre bus trip.

The rather large lady sitting next to me, who was on her way to Albany to visit a friend, was exceptionally talkative; in the course of her non-stop conversation, I learnt that she had lost thirty-five kilos in six months. I could not help but think of my pack, and I tried to imagine what it would be like losing the equivalent of two such packs in six months.

After we had cleared Perth, the driver put on the film *Rocky*. Although I was vaguely aware of the figures moving across the screen at the front of the bus, I was not following the film, otherwise I might have been a little disappointed when, after about half an hour, the video machine suddenly went on strike, and the one and only attempt at on-bus entertainment came to a very abrupt and unfortunate end.

The road from Perth to Albany (the Albany Highway) passes through very few towns. From what I could see from the window of the bus, it did not seem to be much more than a long stretch of sealed road cutting through very typical Australian scenery. The somewhat undulating countryside was extremely dry, with wide, pale beige or brown-red expanses broken only by clumps of ash grey trees, the occasional dried-up dam or an empty creek bed, and it was very obvious that rain was the area's top priority. About an hour into the journey, I noticed an ominous build-up of dark clouds, and I wondered if perhaps the rain from the east had actually managed to follow us all the way to the west.

After about one hundred and sixty kilometres, we made a stop at the roadhouse in Williams, a small town in what is known as the wheat-belt of Western Australia. The town was named after the Williams River, which runs through the area, and in 2005 was home to some three hundred people. From Williams we continued for another thirty kilometres on to Arthur River, also in the wheat belt, where a number of people left the bus. The next stop, almost an hour later, was the small village of Kojonup, by which time the heavens had finally opened to release a deluge of much-needed rain from a sky which, by then, was quite dark and foreboding. The rain continued until just before two, when it gradually eased off; thankfully, the darkness withdrew and blue once more reclaimed the sky.

We turned off the main highway and diverted through Cranbrook, another small community with a few houses and a church. After a few passengers had disembarked, we moved on again and soon rejoined the highway.

Prior to the arrival of Europeans, this part of Western Australia had been inhabited by the Bibbulmun – a people comprising at least one hundred different groups. The well-functioning, if primitive, structure of their society did not allow for chiefs or overlords, and according to the Irish welfare worker Daisy Bates (who spent many years living among the Australian Aboriginal people), they were a non-violent people. Their deity was a serpent god, and they believed that the spirits of the dead were taken to a special place called Kur'an'nup, which was somewhere beyond the ocean to the west. When the Europeans arrived from that direction in their peculiar ships, the Bibbulmun supposed that the strange white people were simply their dead relatives who had returned, and they were, at least initially, very accommodating and friendly.[2]

---

[2] Bates, Daisy. *The Passing of the Aborigines: A Lifetime Spent Among the Natives of Australia.* 1938. In Chapter VII *The Last of the Bibbulmun Race.* Ed. Peter O'Connell. Project Gutenberg, 2004. Australia: http://gutenberg.net.au/ebooks04/0400661.txt

Just after half past two, we reached Mount Barker, a much larger farming community that is also the administrative centre for the shire. When we were driving through the town, I noticed the connecting road to Denmark. Denmark is one of the towns on the Track, and just seeing the name on a road sign sent small butterflies flapping around in my stomach as I realized that in only a matter of days we would be *walking* through that very town.

Not long after leaving Mount Barker, we arrived in Albany.

My first impression of Albany was that it was not particularly large, but I later learnt that it is a reasonably sized city and that it has the honour of being Western Australia's oldest town, beginning life in the early years of the nineteenth century. Spread out demurely around Princess Royal Harbour and looking over King George Sound, it was founded on the basis of its suitability as a port. It is still very much a port city, even though other industries, such as timber, agriculture and tourism are now also important.

Albany Backpackers, where we spent the night of the 18th March, is very close to the Southern Terminus, which is the start of the Walk. It is an old rambling building with colourful scenes painted on all available walls, including those in the bedrooms, and the maze of stairs and corridors put me in mind of how a rabbit burrow might look if I was as small as a rabbit and was able to get inside.

After we had booked into the Backpackers, we left our

packs in our room, which was decorated with mermaids and mermen and things that looked like vertical floating trees, and we walked to the Visitors' Centre at the Southern Terminus.

The Southern Terminus building started life in 1889 as the Albany Railway Station, but it was closed in the late 1970s when it became apparent that it was quicker, and more convenient, to travel by bus from Perth to Albany, and the rail link was discontinued.

While we were registering for the Walk (which is compulsory), we learnt that we would not be able to take a boat from Nullaki to Denmark but would need a taxi to take us around Wilson Inlet. We were still absorbing this information, when the woman looked at us, the slightest hint of a smile lurking around her eyes, and said that another option would be to walk all the way around the inlet on public roads, a distance of about thirty kilometres.

I phoned a taxi company in Denmark, and we arranged that we would be collected a few kilometres past the Nullaki campsite at 9.00 am on the 22nd March. It was extremely difficult making such arrangements in advance – we could only hope that we would be able to get there in time; after all, we did not have a mobile phone, so we would not be able to advise him of any changes to our plans. The distance between Albany and Nullaki is just short of fifty kilometres as the crow flies; following the Track, it is probably closer to seventy kilometres. The question was, of course, whether or not we would manage those seventy kilometres in just a little over three days.

We walked up to the town centre, which is actually quite small, did some shopping at Coles and then ate pizza for dinner. Both of us were anticipating the next day, the first day of our Walk, with much excitement and perhaps the very slightest twinge of apprehension.

The Track between Albany and Hidden Valley

Section One

Albany to Northcliffe

The first section of the Walk, when walking in a south-north direction, is the section Albany to Northcliffe, the horizontal part of the 'L'. This section stretches for almost three hundred and forty kilometres along the southern part of the West Australian coast, running through coastal forests and scrub; it also includes many kilometres of actual beach walking, which is not always as idyllic as it may sound. However, there are countless beautiful spots and a great variety of both flora and fauna.

As far as I know, there is no evidence showing that the Bibbulmun people actually walked over the exact same ground that the Track now covers, although I dare say that it is possible. The name *Bibbulmun* was chosen for the Track to celebrate the Bibbulmun people's custom of walking long distances; walking, after all, was the only method the different groups had of connecting with each other for their many celebrations. Even though we were not participating in any significant celebration, the distances covered were long, so, on some level at least, we did have something in common with the original inhabitants of south-west Western Australia.

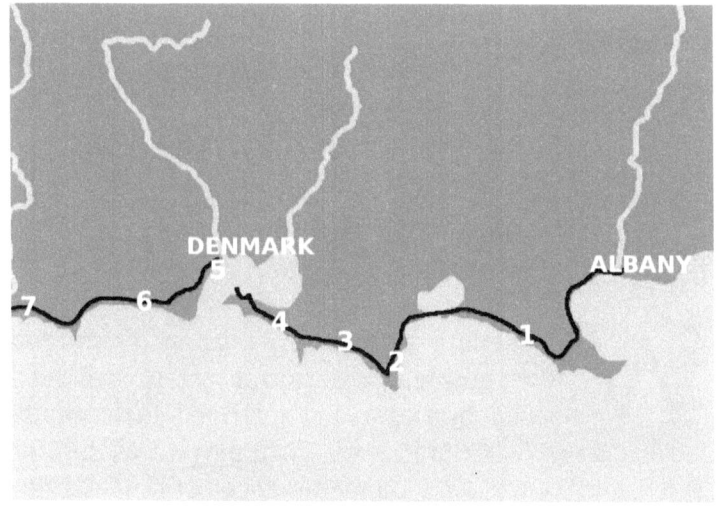

Albany to Boat Harbour 121 kilometres

1 Hidden Valley[3]
2 Torbay
3 West Cape Howe
4 Nullaki
5 *Rivermouth Camping Park, Denmark*
6 William Bay
7 Boat Harbour

(Italics indicate hotel or backpacker accommodation).

---

[3] The Hidden Valley campsite no longer exists (2023), and the section between Albany and Torbay now has two campsites: Sand Patch and Mutton Bird.

Day One
Saturday 19th March

Albany to Hidden Valley

We woke in our beautifully illustrated room to a rather grey and overcast morning. We had a hurried breakfast and managed to leave the Backpackers by six-thirty. It was Saturday, it was the 19th March, and we had 19.3 kilometres ahead of us to the first campsite.

We began by walking the short distance to the Southern Terminus just so that we could say that we had actually started at the official starting point. Once there, we took photos of each other standing near the low red-brown sign with *Bibbulmun Track – Southern Terminus* printed across it in large white letters.

The sleepy morning was still grey and overcast as we took the first steps of the one thousand kilometres stretching out ahead of us. It is fairly obvious that any journey, no matter how long or how short, has to begin with a single step; reduced to basics, a journey or a walk is simply a long series of single steps; in this case, somewhere in the vicinity of two million. Although the number of steps was daunting, the biggest challenge for me was getting used to the weight of the pack. With its

added four litres of water, it was beginning to feel very heavy even before the Southern Terminus was out of sight, and I was seriously wondering what I had let myself in for. A few initial small hills on the edge of the town only helped to intensify the situation, and I was hoping that my back and legs would eventually accept the extra weight; they had always done so in the past, and I told myself that there was no reason why they would not do so now.

The first part of the day's walk, once we had got beyond the town, was along a reasonably flat shoreline that was watched over by the hills of Mount Melville and Mount Clarence. As the morning slowly woke up, the sun began to shine, the greyness dispersed, and everything took on a very different perspective. We walked past the old wool stores, which looked as though they may have been in the process of being pulled down, past the foreshore and, finally, up and on to the ridge. By the time we reached the ridge, we were well and truly out of the town and into the bush. We had already done about twelve kilometres. With only seven left to go to our first shelter, we stopped on the top of the ridge, looking out over the Southern Ocean, and ate some lunch.

The excitement of the adventure had already taken hold, though it was still difficult to fully comprehend that for the next couple of months we would be surrounded only by the outdoors and a wonderful sense of isolation.

In front of us a magnificent wind farm was spread across the headlands, the majestic white structures silhouetted against the stunted, green-grey vegetation of the headland and the varied blues of the ocean. I am fully aware that there are many people who do not like wind turbines, but I have always been fascinated by them, and these ones were no exception. As we came closer to the farm, the Track winding in and out across the ridges, we were constantly treated to many different angles and views of the surreal windmill-like shapes.

We also saw quite a few snakes, and we guessed that the snakes were either tiger snakes or dugites, the ones with the more obvious patterning being the tiger snakes. Both species are quite deadly, so it probably made very little difference to know exactly what they were called (I did ask them, but none of them were at all interested in answering). As well as actually *seeing* snakes, we also heard them rustling through the undergrowth.

Snakes and hiking often go hand in hand, but knowing that Australia has more deadly snakes than any other country is not a particularly comforting thought. Over the years, I have learnt that snakes are usually just as afraid of us as we are of them, and giving them a very wide berth and ignoring them seems to work best. Also, there is not a lot of point in focusing on all the dreadful things that *might* happen (but probably will not happen), otherwise it would be almost impossible to go anywhere outside the dubious concrete safety of the city.

Just after one o'clock in the afternoon, we reached our very first shelter on the Track: Hidden Valley. We had managed our first nineteen kilometres in good time; moreover, I had not succumbed to the weight of the pack, we had not fallen off any of the many cliffs, and we had not got lost.

The shelter was all ours, and as it was delightfully sunny and warm, without a single mosquito anywhere, we both lay down on the floor and slept for at least an hour. Later we made dinner on our very small methylated spirits stove and went to bed early. All night we were treated to the sound of the wind farm, a sound very much like waves breaking on the beach.

Day Two
Sunday 20th March

Hidden Valley to just past Torbay

The following morning, we were up and away early. Although I was still getting used to the weight of the pack, the walking itself was not that difficult, and we were pleased to have managed the seventeen and a half kilometres to Torbay by midday.

All the way from Hidden Valley, the Track skirted the fabulously blue Southern Ocean, the wind farm gradually fading into the haze behind us until it completely disappeared. Sometimes the Track followed the ridge, sometimes it ran along the beach; most of the time it provided us with absolutely amazing views, both to the east behind us and to the west in front of us. Long sweeps of white beach formed a distinctive border to the varied greys and greens of the low coastal vegetation, only to disappear from view where frequent outcrops of bushy tea tree pressed in on the Track from both sides, forming tight corridors.

The tea tree shrub, with its leathery elliptical green-grey leaves and small white flowers (though there were no flowers when we were on the Track), can reach heights of five or six metres. It is both persistent and extremely hardy, often overpowering other vegetation and, in some places, even the Track itself. In the narrow passageways, the branches would sometimes grab and pull at our clothing and our packs; then the bushes would suddenly open up, and the Track would, once again, reclaim its own space.

Besides the thick profusion of tea tree, there were also many scruffy she-oaks with long, thin, untidy needle-like leaves, the grey-green needles clinging to the branches, like drooping feathers on some exotic bird. Many needles had fallen to the ground beneath the trees, creating a soft, quiet carpet on which we walked.

After walking for about eleven kilometres (the last two or three along a long length of sandy beach) we reached Torbay Inlet with just a little trepidation. The information book we were using had warned us about the inlet, and we were expecting some serious wading, but we had a completely dry crossing, which may have depended on the tide being out.

About a kilometre or so before reaching the shelter at Torbay, we encountered the first of many boot-cleaning stations along the Track. A boot-cleaning station is a large metal box with a lid and a hard brush, and we took it in turns to sit on the wooden bench provided and diligently brush the soles of our boots into the box, not an easy feat while still strapped to a pack. The idea with the stations is to try to prevent the spread of a disease known as dieback. Dieback attacks the roots of certain trees, killing them. Over time, with all the trees dead, an area impacted by dieback will be covered by not much more than low vegetation and grasses.

After returning the lid to the box, we continued on to the campsite and the shelter. As we came around the corner of the dark timber building, we saw that someone was sitting at the picnic table, and a few moments later we came face to face with Gordon, the first person we had so far met on the Track.

Gordon was a small, tough-looking man in his early sixties with a long, white-grey beard and long hair of much the same colour. We all introduced ourselves, and Gordon told us that he was from Albany. As he sat at the table, setting up his small stove in order to prepare his meal, he told us about his wife, who had tragically drowned only two years earlier.

Gordon and his wife had been swimming at one of the beaches near Albany when his wife suddenly moved out of her depth and was immediately caught in a rip. From what Gordon told us, the surf zone on many of the local beaches is often littered with sand bars and troughs, which are extremely treacherous: as he put it: "One minute you're touching bottom; the next, you're fighting to keep your head above water."

Sitting on the beach, Gordon's brother-in-law saw what was happening and instantly dived into the water. Although both he and Gordon managed to swim across the rip and pull the poor woman back to shore, it was already too late, and they were unable to resuscitate her.

Not having allowed anyone but his wife to cut his hair, Gordon decided, after her death, that no one would cut his hair any more: he would let it grow long.

This was all we knew about Gordon, but the extent to which the unexpected loss of his wife had impacted on him was very apparent. Apart from his unruly hair and beard, everything about him seemed steeped in the awfulness of what had happened. I suspected that he was hoping that the Walk might help him regain some kind of balance in his life.

Gordon's very sad story definitely dampened the bright colours beyond the campsite and even managed to push away all topics of conversation. This resulted in a dismal kind of silence settling over the three of us as Gordon finished preparing his meal and we started cooking our own dinner; it was difficult to know exactly what to talk about when everyone's thoughts were still trapped on a beach somewhere near Albany.

But then, as the three of us sat around the table to eat, the cloud thankfully lifted, and the colours resumed their normal brightness. Liberated, the conversation drifted around different aspects of life in Albany and Sydney and then fastened on to our varied, individual experiences of the Track. Although it was enjoyable to be able to share some of our impressions with a third person, once Jonathan and I had finished eating and had cleaned up after our meal, we decided that we would move on.

We were fully aware that it was more than sixteen kilometres to the campsite at West Cape Howe, and we had no illusions of reaching the shelter before evening, but we decided we would try to get as far as possible. Having to meet the taxi at Nullaki on the 22nd – not much more than a day hence – was causing us some anxiety, and we wanted to get as as many kilometres behind us as possible. There were still a few hours of daylight left, and it was pleasantly warm.

After leaving Torbay, we saw many shearwaters, also known as muttonbirds. A reasonably large bird, the adults have a wingspan of about one metre and, like the albatross, are amazing fliers. While the name *shearwater* refers to the way they shear across the surface of the water before rising high into the sky, the other name, *muttonbird,* was coined by early European settlers in Australia who killed the birds for their flesh, which is supposed to taste like mutton. The shearwaters migrate every year from the Arctic to nesting colonies south of the Australian mainland; although the bird is now protected, Tasmania still allows an annual commercial killing season in April, during which time up to a quarter of a million birds are killed for their feathers, oil and meat.

As we walked along the ridge, we saw an amazing number of tiny kangaroo ticks, which are very common in this particular area of Western Australia and which can leave a nasty welt if they bite. Although many of them actually fell off bushes as we went past, none of them hung around long enough to bite us.

After about four kilometres from the Torbay campsite, we passed our second boot-cleaning station, by which time it was beginning to get dark.

Without the choice of a good, flat campsite (the ground on either side of the Track was anything but flat), we pitched the tent practically in the middle of the Track itself. As we had already suspected, the tent was way too short for Jonathan, and he spent most of the night with his legs bent up to his chin.

Before leaving on our Walk, we had spent a lot of time debating as to whether or not we would even bring the tent, a two-person hiking tent; after all, it was extra weight to carry, and we had been informed by the

Bibbulmun website and all the information books that there was a shelter at every campsite. However, we had also been advised to bring a tent, just in case a shelter happened to be full. We felt that having a back-up plan made sense, but we only used the tent twice, and, when Andris returned to Sydney at the end of his part of the Walk, he took the tent with him.

Staircase from the beach to the ridge

Day Three
Monday 21st March

West Cape Howe

When we crawled out of our sleeping bags at some unearthly hour the following morning, and more or less fell out of the tent and on to the Track, it slowly dawned on us that it was a Monday. Most people would soon be on their way to work where they would be doing all the fairly ordinary things one does at work, while we were on an unbelievably beautiful stretch of the West Australian coastline where, if we were not actually doing extraordinary things, we were not doing ordinary things. The awareness, though quite obvious, was still exhilarating.

It was not so remarkable that we were up so early: neither of us, especially not Jonathan, had managed to sleep particularly well. We also had Nullaki and the taxi hanging over us. Our goal was to reach West Cape Howe – eleven kilometres further to the west – before midday and then continue on to Nullaki in the afternoon.

All the walking was on top of the ridge, once again with amazing views of the Southern Ocean. I walked first, and initially everything was going really well; in fact, we were making particularly good time. Then, about four kilometres along the Track, we missed a Waugal track sign and ended up on a smaller track leading out towards the edge of the ridge. It took quite some time before we became aware of our mistake, by which time we had almost reached the end of the small track.

Although Waugal sounds as though it could be some kind of bizarre bird, it is actually a yellow triangular sign with a black image of a snake. It is not only a Track marker, it is also the symbol for the Bibbulmun Walk. When the point of the triangle is up, then the track goes straight ahead; when it points towards the left or the right, then the track goes in the same direction. The Waugal, a serpent-like creature, is part of the Aboriginal Dreaming – an endless, timeless state that connects both with creation and the spirits of the ancestors – and was an important deity of the Bibbulmun people. There is a clear association between the Waugal and the land: it was the Waugal who created the hills and the valleys, the rivers and the lakes.

The story behind the sign is definitely interesting and even inspiring. Although, when we found ourselves standing on a wind-swept headland where we should not have been, we were not thinking about stories from the Dreaming. We did, very briefly, consider cutting through the stunted coastal vegetation in the hope of reconnecting with the Track further along towards West Cape Howe, but we soon discarded that idea and retraced our steps.

Not long after getting back on the Track, we reached a bench perched on the ridge. The bench had a beautiful view of the ocean, and we decided to take a break. It was while we were sitting there, contemplating the amazing variety of blues and greens in the water below us, that Gordon caught up to us. We made room for him, and the three of us sat on the bench above the water, admiring the view and talking.

It had turned very warm. Like both the two previous days, there were quite a lot of snakes; there were also many different birds, mainly wrens and finches but even the odd muttonbird.

Our plans to reach the West Cape Howe campsite early and then walk through to Nullaki, which was another sixteen or seventeen kilometres further on, were beginning to unravel, and we were already doubting that they were even feasible. However, if we did not reach Nullaki by evening, we both knew that there was no way that we could possibly meet the taxi at nine the following morning.

Gordon became involved in the discussion; he was completely unaware that the boat across the inlet was not running and that a taxi had to be booked in advance. As he had a mobile phone, he offered to phone the taxi company. Fortunately, he must have had luck on his side, because he was actually able to get a connection, and he easily changed the meeting time to three-thirty in the afternoon. In return for his help, it was decided that he would accompany us to Denmark.

Day Four
Tuesday 22nd March

West Cape Howe to Nullaki to Denmark

After spending the night at West Cape Howe, the three of us set off after breakfast for Nullaki. Once again we were walking along the top of the ridge with fantastic views of the Southern Ocean on our left.

It was an extremely warm day, and the low, open vegetation, with practically no shade, meant that walking soon became quite exhausting. We met no one on the Track, and Gordon was well in front, reaching Nullaki ahead of us. He then left his pack at the shelter and very kindly returned and carried mine for the last couple of kilometres.

It was not quite two o'clock by the time we had all assembled at Nullaki shelter, and we were thankful for a twenty-minute rest in the shade. At some point during those twenty minutes, Gordon took his phone to higher ground and managed to make contact with the taxi driver, who explained where we were to meet up.

We finally strapped on our packs and set out to cover the remaining two kilometres to Eden Road. By now it was really *very* hot, and I was secretly relieved that we did not have that far left to go.

At the beginning of an extension track to Eden Road, Jonathan and Gordon left me minding all the packs, while they went ahead to meet the taxi. I was more than happy to be able to sit on the side of the road in a small patch of shade where, except for the occasional bird and the gentle sounds of small insects, it was wonderfully quiet; actually, it was so quiet that it would have been very easy to have fallen asleep. However, before that happened, the taxi drove in on the extension track. Jonathan jumped out and helped me pile in the three packs, and we then set off for Denmark.

The taxi driver, a pleasant, easy-going man, drove us all to the Rivermouth Camping Park on the other side of the inlet, where Jonathan and I had already pre-booked a cabin. Gordon phoned a friend of his who lived in Denmark and who very soon arrived at the camping area and collected him.

Denmark is a small rural town on the western edge of Wilson Inlet – the inlet over which the boat was not sailing and around which we had to travel by taxi – and it has absolutely nothing to do with the country Denmark. It received its name from the Denmark River, which was named in 1829 by Dr Thomas Braidwood Wilson after naval surgeon Dr Alexander Denmark. Wilson discovered the river while he was exploring the area; in fact, he explored quite a large expanse of the south-west, and many geographical features or places now bear the names of his friends or colleagues. The inlet itself was named after Wilson by the first governor of Western Australia, Governor James Stirling, and there will be more incidental information about him further on.

Both Jonathan and I had quick showers, enjoying the luxury of hot water after four days on the Track, and then hitched into the town with a friendly Indian family who was staying at the caravan park.

The post office had just closed: the post office official had literally only just locked the door and was in the process of pocketing the key when we arrived at the front door. Aware of our disappointment, he very kindly let us in through the back door (I really do not know why he did not simply reopen the front door), and we followed him past the array of things that tend to end up 'out the back' and entered the actual post office area. He found an empty box which I filled with an assortment of things that I had taken from my pack before leaving the caravan park. After four days of walking, there were a number of things that, even if they had been initially considered necessary, had now, mainly on the basis of weight, been drastically demoted to *unnecessary*. The box, when packed, weighed over four kilos, so I was hoping that I would be able to look forward to a slightly lighter pack; I also suspected that, in my haste to reduce weight, I was possibly getting rid of things that I might eventually discover I actually needed.

We then did some shopping at Coles and bought a litre of orange juice, one of my cravings after a few days of walking. We also stocked up on things like jelly beans and jelly snakes. Many walkers swear by trail mix, which usually contains a mixture of different kinds of nuts, dried fruit and chocolate. Some of these mixes also contain seeds and even coconut or ginger. Although we often combine dried fruit and nuts with the jelly beans and snakes, we have found that chocolate is far too dense or heavy when we are actually walking, and we usually only eat it of an evening when we are at the campsite. For us, the very best energy boosters when walking have been things like jelly beans. Nuts and roasted soy beans can be great for lunch or at the end of a day when we have reached the camp.

We are vegetarians, and on this Walk, as on any other Walk we have done, we relied mainly on lentils (both green and red), chick peas, dehydrated vegetables, powdered potato, noodles and a few pre-prepared Indian dinners that only needed to be heated. At the beginning of any day, we would place the lentils or chick peas in a wide-mouthed plastic bottle full of water, and let them soak for the duration of the day's walk. On reaching the campsite, we would replace the water and turn the lentils or peas into a stew or a curry or a soup. We also carried dehydrated soups as a back-up when we needed extra food. Breakfast was oats, and lunch was an assortment of crispbreads with Vegemite or processed cheese, roasted soy beans or, occasionally, leftovers from the previous evening's meal.

My feet by this stage of the Walk were in a rather dreadful state with an array of blisters of differing sizes, and after some searching, we found a chemist. The chemist seemed concerned, but he was not particularly helpful. He suggested a spray normally used for sunburn, which worked as an anaesthetic, and a spray-on bandage that he claimed was specifically for blisters. Although I bought both the sprays, it very soon became quite clear that neither was what I needed, and most probably made the blisters worse than they already were. Eventually, the sprays would be discarded in favour of proper blister care, but when we were in Denmark that moment was still a long way into the future.

I am not sure why I got such dreadful blisters on this Walk: I was wearing a pair of Rossi boots that had already done close to two thousand kilometres; in other words, they were definitely worn in. It is more than likely that the problem was a combination of consistent heat and kilometres of beach walking.

On our walk back to the camping area, we had dinner at a lovely little restaurant: Jonathan had mushroom risotto, and I had leek and potato soup with Parmesan cheese. Red wine together with some very friendly service definitely made the meal a complete success. Afterwards, we walked back to the camping area in the dark, along a track that followed the river. At the cabin, we finished drying our washing, and then we went to bed.

Day Five
Wednesday 23rd March

Denmark to William Bay

When we woke up on the morning of the twenty-third March, we knew that we already had four days behind us and a nineteen-kilometre stretch to the next shelter. What we did not know is that we were about to experience one of the worst days we would experience on the whole of the Track.

Already when we got up, we guessed that it was going to be a hot day, though in hindsight, it was probably good that we had no idea just *how* hot. We should definitely have left the camping area much earlier than we did, but it was already nine by the time we had packed everything together, had eaten breakfast and I had phoned Andris from a telephone near the reception building.

After leaving the Rivermouth Camping Park, it suddenly dawned on us that the actual Track started four kilometres further on, which meant that our anticipated nineteen-kilometre day very quickly become a twenty-three-kilometre day. At the point where the Track began, which was close to where the ferry would have landed had it been operating, we stopped on some soft grass near the water and took a short break.

The grass was a beautiful shade of green, a cross between avocado and olive green, and it was pleasant being able to lie in the shade on the grass while watching some ducks waddling around near the water's edge. But, with the Track waiting, we could only afford to stay there ten minutes before hoisting our packs back on to our shoulders and setting off in a south-west direction towards Mount Hallowell.

Not long after getting back on the Track, we caught up with Gordon. He had obviously made an even later start than we had, given that the friend with whom he had stayed had very kindly driven him to the connection point.

It did not take long before the Track began to climb upwards through a thickly forested and, in parts, rather rocky area. Gordon and Jonathan were so far ahead of me I could no longer see them, and I followed what I believed was a yellow Waugal sign. The sign, however, was minus the snake, so it was not a Waugal sign at all, and I ended up getting completely lost. The track I was following eventually led to a road where there were a few houses but no signs. I asked a young boy on a bike, who came past walking two dogs, if he had any idea where the actual Track was. He was very eager to be of help, and he showed me how I would have to return back up the hill which I just walked down, and then take a turn this way and another turn that way.

I decided to follow his directions, not knowing if the information I had received from him was correct; I had no choice. Even though I was beginning to fear that I really might be lost, I pushed on, trying to remember when to turn this way and when to turn that way. I was completely enclosed by almost impenetrable bush, heat and the monotonous sound of insects, and the first sensations of panic were beginning to rise to the surface. There were still no Waugals, and I had no idea whether I was even going in the right direction.

But then I turned a bend in the track and saw, to my inexpressible relief, that I was back at the point where I had followed the sign without the snake. When I walked a few more metres, I saw the proper yellow Waugal (with a snake), and knew I was on the right Track.

My prayers had been answered, and thoughts of Frederick McCubbin's painting *The Lost Child* slowly faded as I understood that I was not meant to share the same fate as the child in the painting. The Track suddenly seemed somewhat wider and more defined; I saw another Waugal and my spirits rose even higher. I even began to wonder how I could have been so upset. The oven-like heat was pushing in on me from all directions, but it had become secondary to my elation at having found the Track.

There was no one around. I knew that both Gordon and Jonathan would have been several kilometres ahead of me by this stage. Then I began to wonder if they had noticed that I was missing, and, if so, whether or not they were at all concerned. I assumed that they were, and this realization began to stir up the anxiety that I thought had been well and truly put to rest.

It was at this point that I heard a sound on the Track ahead of me: it was obviously someone coming towards me. As I pushed my way through a section of the Track where the vegetation on either side was threatening to reclaim it, I came face to face with Jonathan.

My initial emotion was relief – my anxiety, although well founded, could now finally be put to rest – but there were other emotions as well. I was delighted, upset, apologetic and even somewhat guilty. My appreciation was unable to find all the right words, but I attempted to tell him, as best I could, just how very grateful I was.

Jonathan told me that when he realized that I was not behind him he had left his pack by the side of the Track and had come back looking for me. He shrugged off my apologies, reminding me that it was fairly easy to lose the Track, something we had both done on a few occasions already. He then took my pack, and we walked for at least two or three kilometres, first through encroaching vegetation and, finally, over a tediously long stretch of very steep, stony ground to where he had left his pack.

It was becoming hotter and hotter (we later learnt that the temperature that day reached 42°C), but there was really nothing we could do about it. We had no choice as we had to get to the campsite, so we trudged onwards, over Mount Hallowell (282 metres) and past a series of granite outcrops, where we observed that we still had eleven kilometres to go. To be perfectly honest, at that stage, all I really felt like doing was lying down on the ground and dying; I did not believe that there was any way I could take another step.

42°C is hot even when lying completely prone in protective shade while sipping long, icy-cold drinks; however, now there was little shade, definitely no long, cold drinks, and a pack weighing somewhere between twenty and thirty kilos, depending on whether it was mine or Jonathan's. It was not possible to simply lie down and die, so we did the only thing that was possible and kept going.

At a fenced property we crossed a stile into private property, and a little further on we crossed a second one. The three or four steps up to the top of the fence and the same on the other side, coupled with my fear of heights, the heat and the weight of the pack, was almost too much. As we moved on to a ridge above the ocean, I was close to tears, and Jonathan suggested that he could go on ahead of me; once he had left his own pack at the shelter, he would come back along the Track and give me a hand with my pack.

Some time after he left, I was walking along the side of a cliff, with the ocean below me, when I met an elderly couple coming up from Lights Beach. At that point I still had about four and a half kilometres left to the campsite.

The couple mentioned that they had met a lovely young boy about twenty minutes earlier. Understanding that they were most probably referring to Jonathan, there being no other soul anywhere on the Track or elsewhere, I explained that he was my son.

After a few pleasantries, they both exclaimed over the dreadful heat and said that it must be awful having to walk any distance in such weather: they were finding the short walk back up from the beach sufficiently difficult. The lady, who quite obviously was very kind and who probably wanted to make things seem just a little easier than they were, suggested that it might rain the next day, but the man, who no doubt was more realistic, shook his head and said that he reckoned that it was going to be another scorcher.

The couple disappeared towards their parked car, and I continued along the Track until I reached a dirt road that was obviously used by four-wheel drive vehicles. Apart from the fact that the surface was very uneven with long wheel ruts of varying widths, the walking was reasonably good; then I missed the Waugal sign to the right and followed the road to its very end. It came out on to a path which, in turn, led down to a beach. When I saw the end of the road and the beach, my heart dropped, as I knew that I must have missed a sign. Yet again, I had ended up on the wrong track.

Even though late afternoon was beginning to paint the sky liberally with greys and mauves, it was still extremely hot. Moreover, I was completely alone in the middle of what seemed like nowhere, an understanding that was not particularly uplifting. I knew that I would have to retrace my steps, which I did, and eventually I found the sign I had missed.

As I stood at the sign, the colour visibly draining from everything around me, I knew that I was faced with a dilemma: if Jonathan had managed to reach the shelter and was on his way back to find me, he may have already passed the sign on the vehicle track, and could well be on his way towards Lights Beach looking for me.

I considered writing a note to Jonathan, affixing it to the sign and then retracing my steps towards Lights Beach, but I decided that this would be quite stupid if he had not yet passed the turn-off; it would simply mean that he would have further to walk (as would I). So I sat at the intersection and waited. It was now almost dark; the moon, a full moon, was rising and there was a balmy breeze blowing.

Fortunately, I made the right decision, because not long afterwards, Jonathan turned up with a water bottle and two torches. He came from the direction of the campsite, so I was very relieved that I had not opted to retrace my steps towards Lights Beach. Jonathan told me that he had completely run out of water about three kilometres from the shelter and that he had more or less crawled for at least a kilometre until he had finally unstrapped his pack, left it by the side of the Track and walked on to fetch water. After Jonathan set off to find me, Gordon, who had already reached the shelter, went back along the Track and collected the pack for him. As Gordon told me later, he could barely carry it.

Even Gordon had had a dreadful day. From the four-wheel drive track, he had also missed the sign to the right and, like me, had continued all the way to the end of the road. He had then followed the path down to the beach, and was seriously considering the possibility of camping on the beach; he did not have a tent, but it was very warm. When a man turned up in a car and offered to drive him up the hill, Gordon weighed up the pros and cons and decided that he had probably done enough walking for one day and gratefully accepted the lift. As a result he arrived at the campsite via a vehicle track on the northern side of the site.

Jonathan and I walked about three kilometres in the moonlight: we stumbled over rocks, trudged through forests and blundered across sand dunes. Although the dreadful heat had finally gone out of the day, it was still warm; it was also quite dark, but the full moon and the light from the torches meant that we had a fairly good idea of where we were going. When we were about a kilometre from the campsite, we were somewhat startled to see a figure coming towards us before realizing that it was Gordon. The three of us then continued on towards the shelter. As it came into view, we saw a snake, by which time we were all too tired to do much more than mentally note that we had seen a snake.

We were, in fact, totally exhausted. Gordon had already eaten, but Jonathan and I had one of our easy heat-up dinners, and then we crawled into our sleeping bags and fell soundly asleep.

Day Six
Thursday 24th March

William Bay to Peaceful Bay to Rame Head

It dawned grey and overcast, the morning fixed in some limbo zone, undecided as what to do next. All three of us were hoping that it would not be as hot as the previous day, but my thoughts kept going to back to what the man at Lights Beach had said about the continuing hot spell. We packed up early, and a slight breeze started to blow as we were heading towards the beach along the vehicle track. So far, the weather was still reasonably pleasant, but we all knew that at least seven kilometres of the day's walking would be along the beach.

Beach walking can be decidedly difficult. Even minus boots and a pack, a much greater effort is required, and leg muscles and tendons usually get a very good work-out. The weight of a full pack means that feet, with or without boots, tend to sink into the soft sand and an extra effort is then needed to pull them up and take the next step. Seeking out the harder, wet part of the beach does not always alleviate the problem, and when sand lodges in boots and socks (which it does) there is a heightened danger of blisters. The horizon in front and behind, in fact, the entire landscape, never seems to change. At times it feels as though you are walking up and down in the same spot, looking at the same patch of sand, focusing on the same piece of hazy horizon.

When we reached Mazzoletti Beach, it was deserted, except for a four-wheel drive vehicle that was obviously stuck in the sand. I was walking ahead, while Jonathan and Gordon were some way behind. I stopped and spoke with the owner of the vehicle, but he did not seem overly worried by the situation. As he pointed out, he had all the necessary equipment to get himself out of trouble. Some time later, he drove past and indicated that he had received help from the two people behind me.

Jonathan soon caught up to me and then passed me, while Gordon remained well and truly behind us. I think he may have even stopped to have a rest, because after a short while he completely disappeared from sight: all that was visible both behind us and in front of us was an infinite expanse of empty, white sand and, on its edge, the white-crested, blue-green ocean. Two long, parallel indentations in the sand showed us where the four-wheel drive vehicle had been driven; the vehicle itself was nowhere to be seen.

We reached Parry Inlet and crossed it with no problem at all; we did not even have to remove our boots. In fact, it was not until we checked our map that we realized that we had actually crossed it. Then, at Parry Beach Caravan Park, we were told that the Track was closed all the way from Parry Beach to Peaceful Bay because of a bush fire that had been caused by lightning.

This was not something we had been expecting, and we really did not know what we should do. Looking at the map, the only alternative that we could see was to walk around the road, some thirty to thirty-five kilometres, unless, of course, we were prepared to swim around the coast. We decided that the swim, complete with possible sharks and other nasties, was really not an option. The only information we could get about the road walk (Parry Road, the South Coast Highway and Peaceful Bay Road) was that there was a campsite, with a toilet but no shelter, somewhere adjacent to the public road. No one could tell me exactly *where* the campsite was situated and whether or not there was any water there, and I was not prepared to take the risk. It was still extremely warm, and neither of us was prepared to walk all of those thirty-five kilometres in one day, on top of the ten we had already walked. Also we were understandably concerned as to what would do should we arrive the campsite only to find that there was no water.

I spoke to the caretaker of the Parry Beach Caravan Park. He was a rather slow-spoken man; at times, I found it difficult to know whether he was still considering my question or had mentally already moved on to something else. After some discussion as to what we should or should not do, he suggested that we could call CALM[4].

Unfortunately, there was no one there who could give me any kind of advice regarding an alternative route. As could well be expected, with the bush fire still raging, everyone had much more important things to worry about. The man at CALM did, however, suggest that we should try to get a lift with someone from the caravan park.

---

[4] CALM used to be the acronym for Conservation and LandManagement authority; in 2013, CALM became DPW – Department of Parks and Wildlife.

A friendly couple, who were friends of the caretaker, agreed to take us to Peaceful Bay in return for fuel money. As it turned out, the exceptionally long detour would have been a dreadful, non-scenic, hot, dusty, hard, thirsty walk, and it did not take long before we were completely certain that we had made the right, and possibly only, decision. I have no memory of seeing any campsite, but it is possible that it was set back and was not visible from the road.

When we arrived at the Peaceful Bay Caravan Park, we very gratefully paid the couple what we owed them, and then we parted company. We found the caravan park kiosk and bought something to drink, some food and a phone card. Then I phoned home.

Before we actually arrived at Peaceful Bay, Jonathan had been positively anticipating the prospect of checking back into some form of refined living; however, the few days on the Track had blurred the concept, and he said later that he was markedly disappointed by the reality.

Perhaps a caravan park, which is all there is at Peaceful Bay, with lots of people intent on escaping the restraints of the city is not the best place against which to measure the pros and cons of a developed society. The gaudy trappings of what we might call progress are still present, offering some vague security while possibly obliterating the underlying need for the escape.

The day was wearing on, and we still had ten kilometres to the Rame Head campsite. Shouldering our packs, we set off along the Track, first in a southerly direction to Point Irwin and then in a westerly direction to the campsite. The

Track hugged the coast all the way, providing us, as always, with some fantastic views of the ocean.

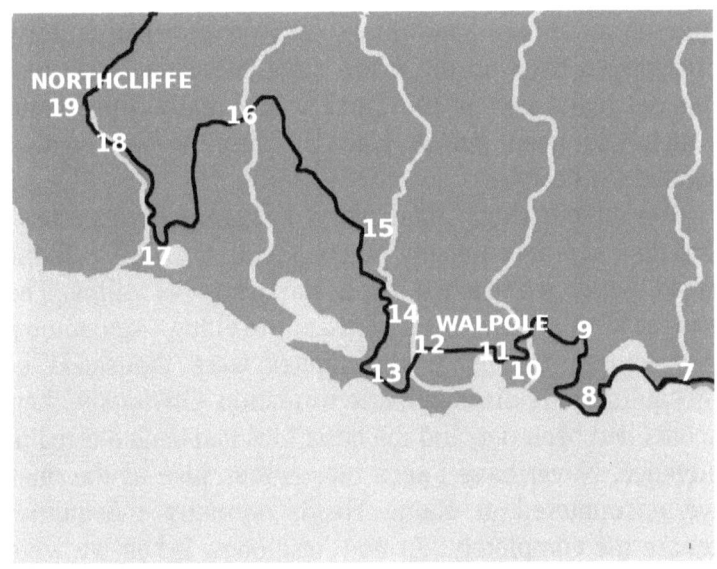

<u>Boat Harbour to Northcliffe 215 kilometres</u>

7	Boat Harbour	14	Woolbales
8	Rame Head	15	Mount Chance
9	Giants	16	Dog Pool
10	Frankland	17	Maringup
11	*Coalmine Beach*	18	Gardner
12	Mount Clare	*19*	*Northcliffe*
13	Long Point		

(Italics indicate hotel or backpacker accommodation).

It was still warm, but nowhere near as hot as it had been the previous day. We crossed many little beaches and rocky headlands before leaving the beach area, about a kilometre from Rame Head. The Track then continued through an area of sand dunes covered with native grass and moved back up on to the ridge. We later learnt that this particular part of the Track was actually a diversion which had been put in place because of bad erosion around the beaches.

Up on the ridge, there were kangaroos everywhere, and they kept us company practically all the way to Rame Head, which we reached just as darkness was falling. The kangaroos may have been pleasant travelling companions, but waiting for us at the shelter were thousands of mosquitoes all poised in battle formation. Obviously, their scouts had been out, and the battalions had been alerted in advance. Never have I seen mosquitoes such as the ones we encountered at Rame Head; normally mosquitoes ignore me completely but not these ones. When we were caught up in the battle, it was a bit like a scene from a horror film.

I am not sure why mosquitoes bite some people and not others. I have heard that it may have something to do with blood types: one theory is that mosquitoes prefer type O (which I am not) over either type A or type B. Another theory is that mosquitoes are attracted to people with sweet-tasting skin, and perhaps I do not fall into that category either. However, the mosquitoes at Rame Head were obviously starving, and they were prepared to take whatever they could get – A, B, AB or O, sweet or otherwise.

Forgetting the mosquitoes for a moment (if that is

possible) the Rame Head shelter is in a wonderful position on the top of a ridge from where there are astonishing views over the ocean; it was just a pity that we were unable to properly enjoy what was on offer.

After we had eaten dinner, I decided to wash some of our clothes, which was undeniably an insane, spur-of-the-moment decision. Even though it was still quite warm, I should have known that it was most unlikely that anything would dry overnight. In an effort to save water, I put the clothes, washing powder and water into a large plastic bag and then shook it vigorously in a rather primitive imitation of a washing machine. With no hands free to defend myself, I was almost eaten alive by the very persistent mosquitoes. Perhaps if I had not been under attack, I may have been able to wring things out better than I did, and perhaps there might have been a small chance that some things may have dried; as it turned out, nothing did dry, so we were left with a pile of half-dry clothes that we had to wrap in plastic and carry to the next campsite.

Gordon was no longer with us. We had not seen him since the early part of Mazzoletti Beach. We had no idea what he had decided to do regarding the closed-off Track; all we could do was to hope that, wherever he was, he was all right.

Day Seven
Friday 25th March

Rame Head to Giants

It was Good Friday and the start of Easter; this meant that for the next few days we would probably be seeing more people both on the Track and in the shelters. We had been enjoying the isolation of the Track - it really felt as though we owned all the wonderful coastal area through which we had been walking – so we were not exactly looking forward to being inundated by lots of weekend walkers. On the more positive side, we knew that we had a short walking day in front of us (a little over fifteen kilometres), and we were hoping that there would be no more unexpected diversions.

It was already quite warm when I left the shelter a good thirty minutes before Jonathan; my main priority was to put the hordes of small bloodthirsty vampires well and truly behind me. From the ridge, with incredible views in all directions, the Track eventually wound down towards the beach, by which time Jonathan had caught up to me. Once on the beach, we were faced with a lot of serious sand and dune walking.

Scrambling up, or down, a sand dune with a full pack can be a rather frustrating pastime. As well as all the usual problems associated with sand or beach walking, there are the special problems associated with sand dunes.

We soon discovered that it could be extremely difficult to get a foothold in the dry, slippery sand, and, when we were not sliding backwards to where we had begun, our feet would often sink up to our ankles. At other times, as we were navigating a particularly steep ascent or descent, the weight of the pack could easily throw us off balance without warning.

However, we persevered and, after crossing the dunes, finally climbed up on to the ridge above Conspicuous Bay. The name was interesting, and we both wondered what was so conspicuous about the bay; however, I have since learnt that it is actually a limestone cliff overlooking the bay, and not the bay itself, that was deemed conspicuous.

It was here, on top of the ridge, that we once again lost the Track. This time, though, it was not completely our fault, as the information in the guide book was rather inconclusive. Losing the Track caused us to walk a long way along a gravel road before it occurred to us that we were actually no longer on the Track, at which point we had no choice other than to return to where we had started. Given the fact that 'quite warm' was now 'very warm', we were not too happy about the extra kilometres, but once we were back at the starting point above Conspicuous Bay, we resorted to some brilliant detective work that would have been worthy of Agatha Christie's Hercule Poirot, and we soon picked up the Track on a parallel hill.

At many points along the Track, we were able to look back east in the direction from where we had come, and we could marvel at the fact that we had actually walked so far, the headlands and ridges, that we had already crossed, disappearing well beyond the horizon. We calculated that we must have walked at least one hundred and fifty kilometres, and even if we had lost thirty kilometres on account of the fire, we were quite certain that we had made up those kilometres, and possibly more, with all the wrong turns we had made and all the backtracking we had had to do.

The Track, now moving in a northerly direction, wound inland through areas that were both swampy and sandy; it also crossed several small creeks and a number of old vehicle tracks. As it moved further away from the coast, the vegetation became taller and the shade more reliable. On one short section, we walked through hundreds of spider webs stretched across the path. The webs were very fine, and many of them were filled not only with small insects, which is why they were there in the first place, but also with some very big spiders.

We continued until we reached the edge of a large forest where, with a little imagination, it was easy to believe that we were walking into some kind of fairy story. There was still a lot of low coastal vegetation mixed in with the taller jarrah and tingle trees, but the shape of the forest was there, with its illusion of trolls and other forest dwellers. Slightly further along the Track, the forests would become completely dominated by these trees and the even larger karri, creating the background for a southern-hemisphere variation of all the well-known fairy tales.

All three trees – tingle, jarrah and karri – belong to the eucalyptus family, with the tingle (around seventy-five metres in height) and the giant karri (eighty metres) dwarfing the shorter, forty-metre-high jarrah. Jarrah is not only extremely common in this south-west area of Western Australia, it is one of the trees most susceptible to dieback, which is a cause of growing concern and the motivation behind the many boot-cleaning stations. The rather rough and stringy bark varies in colour from taupe grey to taupe brown and has a tendency to peel off from the tree in long strips, not in patches as is the norm with most other eucalyptus trees.

Only to be found in this part of Western Australia, the tingle is the longest living eucalypt in the world. Further along the Track, in the Valley of the Giants, there are tingle trees that date back to the beginning of the seventeenth century, long before European settlement in Australia.

As we entered the forest, a fine, misty rain began to fall, which was a welcome relief after the unrelenting heat of the day. We covered our packs but did not worry about rainwear for ourselves, enjoying instead the soft, wet coolness on our faces and arms.

Further into the forest, we saw a small animal sitting on the Track. It was quite tiny and grey, and we assumed that it was some kind of mouse. When it became aware of us standing and watching it, it scurried away very quickly, disappearing into the undergrowth. We later learnt that it was most probably not a mouse at all but a mardo. Mardos are grey marsupials that look a little like mice, and the males follow such a frenetic mating pattern that few of them ever live past their first birthday. Although the mardo was the only animal we saw, there were a lot of small wren-like birds in the trees and bushes.

It was just after four in the afternoon when we finally reached the Giants campsite in the middle of the forest. A young couple, who introduced themselves as Rebecca and Patrick, had already arrived at the camp and were in the process of putting up their tent. They told us that they were doing a short two-to-three-day hike, in a south-north direction. As they were using a tent, Jonathan and I were the only two people in the shelter. We stretched a line across the inside of the shelter and hung up our still rather damp washing from Rame Head. Later, minus the mosquitoes and the blistering heat of the past few days, we both slept really well.

Day Eight
Saturday 26th March

Giants to Frankland

We had already planned this day as a very short walk (barely fourteen kilometres), with the idea of spending some time at the Tree Top Walk in the Valley of the Giants.

For the first time on the Walk, the weather was slightly cooler, and as it was not raining it was ideal walking weather. Heading in a westerly direction, we were at the Tree Top Walk well before it opened at nine.

The Tree Top Walk is a six-hundred-metre walk, forty metres above the ground in the canopy of tingle trees. Even with my horror of heights, I actually appreciated the feeling of being so high up, protected as I was on both sides by a secure wire fence. I wondered if the sensation of being surrounded by the tops of trees could possibly be compared with the way birds might feel when they look down on the world below them.

As well as the actual Tree Top Walk there is also a ground walk through giant trees that are hundreds of years old; in fact, the tingle and many of the other plants in the area have been traced back more than two hundred million years to the Gondwana supercontinent. It was both exciting and humbling to be so close to the descendants of a time span that is difficult, if not impossible, to conceive.

There were only a few other people at the park when it opened, which meant that we were able to do the Tree Top Walk in relative solitude. Afterwards, with our feet once again in contact with the ground, we strolled around the giant red tingles in what is called the Ancient Empire Walk. This walk, part of which is on a boardwalk, winds in and out of, and even through, some of the giant trees, many of which measure more than fifteen metres in circumference at the base. The very large base area is due to a natural buttressing that the tree uses to rectify a relatively shallow root system, and the heavy, gnarled supports lean in towards the trunk like closely linked circles of weighty security guards. The trees, which have a definite reddish tinge, manage to fill the forest space both horizontally and vertically, and I doubt that anyone would question as to why they are called giants.

It would have been pleasant to have been able to spend more time in the park, but we did not want to be arriving at the shelter too late in the day, so we finally left the Tree Tops and returned to the Track.

Despite a few hilly sections, this day was probably our easiest walking day so far: the ground, carpeted with a variety of fallen leaf matter, was delightfully soft underfoot, the forest was pleasantly cool, and the Track itself moved fairly consistently westwards, without too many loops, twists or turns. There were many small creeks and waterways, and everywhere there were birds and birdsong. I recognized wrens, finches and tits, though there were also a number of other small birds, the names of which I did not know.

Not long after crossing the Frankland River, we arrived at Frankland. Both Frankland and the Frankland

River were named in 1829 by the explorer Dr Thomas Braidwood Wilson, whom I have already mentioned in association with Denmark and the Wilson Inlet. Wilson chose the name *Frankland* in honour of George Frankland, who had been appointed Surveyor General of Tasmania the previous year.

It was still early afternoon, and the campsite was deserted except for the two of us. We swept the shelter thoroughly, established our sleeping mats and packs in an inner corner, filled in the register and then organized our meal.

During the afternoon, people started dropping in (as we had more or less expected), and we were soon sharing the space with at least fifteen people. This was a new, and fairly startling, experience for us: up until now we had only ever had to share a shelter with one other person, Gordon.

When Rebecca and Patrick arrived, they took one look at the shelter, shook their heads and proceeded to put up their tent.

Among the other visitors to the shelter, there was a mother with two teenage sons; a fellow with a tight little beanie who had once been in the army and who told us (and everyone else) that he knew absolutely everything and anything that was even vaguely worth knowing about camping, hiking and trekking; his girlfriend, who had a high, shrill voice that made her sound as though she was about ten even though she was most certainly a good deal older; a Japanese girl with very tight, very clean, designer jeans and beautifully styled hair; and an extremely worried-looking young man who was huddled in a corner, most probably wishing that everyone would move out of the shelter and give him more room. Although I was able to sympathize with his obvious concerns regarding the space, I knew that there was very little anyone could do to change the situation.

I was sincerely hoping that everyone was heading south, not north, and that they would all be moving on to Giants the following day.

The campsite toilets had so far been clean and well cared for by those using them, but the toilet at Frankland was absolutely disgusting!

Day Nine
Sunday 27th March

Frankland to Walpole

It was Easter Sunday, and we were up well and truly before the kookaburras' peals of laughter cut through the early-morning darkness. Kookaburras, related to the kingfisher, can only be found in Australia and New Guinea, and the name comes from a Wiradjuri word *guuguubarra*, which is an attempt to mimic the bird's very strange call. The birds are usually heard fifteen minutes before sunrise and, again, fifteen minutes before sunset.

    Carefully stepping over and around all the prone bodies, we somehow got ourselves and our packs out of the shelter without waking anyone. We found a grassy spot, between some trees and away from the shelter, where we sorted our packs and ate our breakfast. Well before eight o'clock, we were on the Track and heading for Walpole.

    Walpole was named after the Walpole Inlet which, in turn, was named after the Walpole River. The river was discovered in 1831, not by the intrepid Dr Wilson but by Captain Thomas Bannister. It seems as though Captain Bannister gave the honour of naming the river to

Governor Stirling, who named it after a Captain W. Walpole, with whom he had served on HMS Warspite in 1808.

Situated at the top of the Walpole Inlet, Walpole is quite small with just a few streets, a town park and not much more. I believe that it was established in the 1930s for families from the city who had been badly affected by the Depression. As well as being one of the few towns on the Bibbulmun Track, it now acts as a base for tourists wishing to explore the area.

Initially, after leaving Frankland, we walked in a south-westerly direction which at times was probably more southerly than westerly. There was a quite a lot of uphill walking, but a gentle breeze was blowing, and it was not too hot. On the whole, the walking was pleasant, very much like the previous day, and we passed through many karri, tingle and she-oak forests.

We finally left the forest not far from Hilltop Lookout where we stopped for a short break, enjoying the fantastic views across Nornalup Inlet. The inlet is a large, almost round body of water which, at its southern end, opens into the Southern Ocean via a narrow channel. At its northern end, it opens, via a slightly wider channel, into the Walpole Inlet.

In the local Noongar language, *Nornalup* means 'place of the black snake' or 'place of the tiger snake', but even though we kept a very good watch, as we had done during all of the Walk so far, we saw neither tiger snakes nor black snakes.

We did not stay long at the lookout: we enjoyed the view, took a few photos and then continued on to

Coalmine Beach Caravan Park.

Walpole Inlet

The closer we came to the beach and to the caravan park, we noticed how the scenery gradually reverted to what would be termed *coastal:* there were lots of sand dunes and native grasses and the vegetation was both sparse and stunted.

We had pre-booked a cabin at the caravan park, but because we were actually not expected until the following day the cabin was not available. Instead, we paid for a tent place, Jonathan put up the tent, and, leaving our packs in the tent, we walked the remaining two or three kilometres into Walpole. As could have been expected, we managed to take a wrong turn just past the camping area and walked much further than we need have done, but we eventually reached Walpole where we did some shopping. Later, we went to a pizzeria and had dinner.

After our meal, we walked back to the camping area (without any wrong turns) and went to bed. Not only was the caravan park extremely noisy with all the Easter-holiday campers, it was also very hot. Neither of us was able to sleep, and Jonathan got up in the middle of the night to go for a walk around the grounds. He returned, though, when it began raining, and the rain continued to fall for the rest of the night.

Day Ten
Monday 28th March

Walpole

Today was our very first walk-free day, in fact, it was our *only* walk-free day; it was also the day that Andris was to join us. With a whole day in one place, I had decided to wash our sleeping bags, as well as our clothing, and air all the wet-weather gear. Jonathan managed to get time on the Internet, as he had some work to do, and I later caught up with my note-taking.

The day was pleasantly warm, sunny and very lazy. Earlier in the day we had moved into the cabin, which had become available. Even though we missed the solitude and the isolation of the shelters, the cabin was a luxurious change after almost two weeks of sleeping on bare boards and preparing food on a picnic table. As well as a living room and small kitchen, the cabin had two bedrooms, a bathroom and, at the front, a small veranda.

I finished the washing, thankful that the warm weather meant that everything would dry quickly. Then I also borrowed the Internet at the office and sent a few short emails to people at home. Jonathan read for a while and later walked into Walpole on his own to do some more shopping and also to meet Andris, who was arriving from Perth via Bunbury in the late afternoon. While he was away, I attended to my toes, which, in spite of the two sprays, were beginning to look quite dreadful.

Jonathan arrived back at the caravan park with Andris just after five. I was totally shocked when they walked into the cabin; in the couple of weeks since I had last seen Andris, he had aged at least ten years: his face was grey and drawn, and he was obviously totally exhausted. Jonathan was carrying his pack for him, and all he had was a small day pack, which seemed far too much for him. As he came in through the door, I could see that he was already looking for somewhere to sit. I wondered what on earth had happened; my immediate feeling was that there was absolutely no way he would be able to manage the Walk the following day.

Once Andris had sat down and removed his day pack, and I had got him something to drink, he told me that our daughter and one-year-old grandson, who had been staying with him for a week prior to the family's relocation overseas, had both come down with what our daughter believed was some kind of food poisoning. However, after he had arrived in Perth the previous evening, he had become quite ill with dreadful diarrhoea and vomiting and had spent most of the night in the bathroom. It was then that it occurred to him that it had probably not been food poisoning at all but, in all likelihood, a rather nasty virus.

In the morning, after not having slept a wink all night, and still feeling really dreadful, he got completely lost trying to get to the central station. When he finally found the station and had taken himself the few stations to East

Perth, he was told that the train to Bunbury was not running and that he would have to take a bus all the way to Walpole. Initially, he was unable to find the bus terminal, but then he fortunately connected with a man, who, like him, had also expected to be taking the train to Bunbury, and together they were able to find the terminal without further problem.

He was unable to eat anything, and I was already planning an extra day in Walpole, moving days and distances around in my head. He began to unpack his pack but then collapsed on to the sofa bed in the living room and almost immediately fell asleep. Jonathan and I discussed different alternatives for the next few days, finished sorting a few things, and then we too went to bed.

Day Eleven
Tuesday 29th March

Walpole to Mount Clare

Although Andris looked ever so much better in the morning, I still felt that we should remain in Walpole another day to give him time to recover completely. I told him as much, several times, but he insisted that he was well enough to set out on the Walk. In the end I decided that it was really up to him because no one else could know exactly how he was really feeling.

We packed up and managed to get away from the caravan park by eight o'clock, heading along the Track in a northerly direction towards Walpole. The first two kilometres into town were quite level, and with the weather being extremely pleasant I began to relax. The total walking for the day was only twelve kilometres, and there was no indication that it would be in any way difficult, even though it was apparent from the guide book that there was a slight ascent after Walpole.

There is no hospital in Walpole but there *is* a nursing centre. I was trying to convince myself that everything would eventually right itself with my feet, but both Andris and Jonathan were concerned that a couple of my toes might actually fall off in the interim, and after some fairly heated discussion they eventually persuaded me to call in at the nursing centre on our way through Walpole. The Silver Chain Nursing Centre was housed in a neat little house on Nockolds Street; while I was there, Andris and Jonathan took time out in the town park opposite.

Maureen, the Silver Chain nurse, took one look at my toes and told me that I should not be doing any walking whatsoever, and straight away she gave me a tetanus injection. As she bustled around, she talked about the woes of dune and sand walking, and she told me that in her time at the Centre she had seen a number of walkers with feet looking much the same as mine. When the doctor arrived, he agreed with Maureen: they both felt that I should discontinue the Walk. For me, the idea was impossible, and I told them that it was completely out of the question. After a few moments of reflection, the doctor suggested that I try walking in sandals for a few days. By the time I left the Centre with a prescription for antibiotics, I had had several toenails removed and seven toes bandaged with Fixomull.

I had never heard of Fixomull before, but after an hour at the Silver Chain Nursing Centre I knew that there was absolutely nothing else that should be used for blisters. It is an adhesive bandage or tape that was original designed for burns, and it lets out moisture without letting any in. Now, ten years later, I would not go on any kind of long walk without a good supply of Fixomull; I learnt the hard way that blister pads and cushions, not to mention sprays, are more or less useless.

I fetched the antibiotics from the Chemist, hoping that I would not have to take them, as antibiotics and I usually do not see eye to eye. Andris offered me his sandals, which he had brought with him to use around the campsite, but by some unimaginable stroke of luck I actually managed to find similar sandals at the Walpole general store. While I was looking for sandals, Andris had my camera card downloaded on to a disc, and by eleven we were ready to set off a second time.

It was now very much warmer, around 30°C.

After leaving the town, the Track swung due west and continued in that direction all the way to Mount Clare. Close to Walpole, the ground was still sandy with low vegetation and many clumps of sword grass, which is a type of grass with very strong blades that can grow to about a metre in height, and it was while navigating this part of the Track that we finally saw two tiger snakes. With the name of the area now validated, we pushed on and soon passed through an area of paperbarks, which are medium-sized trees covered with a light-coloured papery bark that easily peels off. The Track then crossed a couple of small creeks, after which the tingle and karri forest began to dominate.

Everywhere we were surrounded by bird life, mainly rosellas and green parrots, but also many small finch-like birds. As had been the case for all of the Walk so far, we had the Track completely for ourselves; except for the birds and the insects and the sounds of our boots on the Track, everything was perfectly still and quiet. Before beginning the Walk, Jonathan and I had made a unanimous decision not to have any kind of portable CD player with us as neither of us could see a lot of point in surrounding ourselves with natural quietness only to plug our ears with constant sound.

A few kilometres beyond Walpole, we caught up with the only two people we were to see on the Track that day. Rob and his son, Chris, from Perth were doing a five- or six-day walk to Northcliffe and, like us, were aiming for Mount Clare.

As the day wore on, the heat began to take its toll on Andris. He may have begun the day quite positive about managing the twelve kilometres to Mount Clare, but he was actually still very weak, and the events of the last couple of days were now beginning to catch up with him. Although he had seemed a good deal better in the morning, by early afternoon, he was beginning to look quite awful again.

Mount Clare

Jonathan kindly took some of the things from his father's pack, which made the walking a little easier for him, and after a number of short and medium rest breaks we arrived at the Mount Clare shelter around three in the afternoon.

The campsite is situated in the middle of a beautiful tingle and karri forest, and Rob and Chris, who had arrived some time before us, had already claimed their part of the shelter and were relaxing in the sun.

Our initial plan, before Andris became ill, had been to hop over Mount Clare and continue on to Long Point; however, even had Andris been well, I doubt that it would have been such a good idea. Jonathan and I had already been walking for almost two weeks and had more or less got used to the weight of our packs; for Andris, it was his very first day on the Track.

The camping place among the enormous karri and tingle trees was extremely pleasant, though the leaves from the trees did tend to give the tank water a slightly brownish appearance. It tasted all right, as long as we closed our eyes.

We quickly organized our places in the shelter and then made dinner, while a rather curious crow paid very close attention to what we were doing. Afterwards, we spent some time talking with our new friends, and then all of us, including the crow, went to bed just after the onset of darkness.

Day Twelve
Wednesday 30th March

Mount Clare to Long Point

We were out of our sleeping bags early, but it had begun to rain heavily well before we were ready to leave the shelter. We waited, hoping that there would be a break in the rain, but when that did not happen we changed into wet-weather gear (which meant that I had to get back into my boots).

After some time, the rain eased off a little, and we left the shelter, following the Track as it descended in a southerly direction towards the coast. Eventually, on reaching the coast, the Track would again turn towards the west and the Long Point campsite.

It was extremely pleasant in the forest, admittedly somewhat damp and slippery after the rain, but still quite fresh and invigorating. Also, my feet were feeling better than they had for several days, in spite of being back in boots. As we came closer to the coast, we began to move out of the forest and into dune country from where we were able to catch magnificent views of the ocean and the ridges.

Walking along the open, more or less treeless, ridge, we paralleled the beach area for some distance. It was while we were walking there that it suddenly began to rain again, and we were all rather thankful that we were still wearing wet-weather gear. When the rain eased off after about ten minutes, none of us dared express the hope that this might be the end of the rain, for fear of jinxing ourselves.

Whether it was our fault or not, it is difficult to say, but thirty minutes had not passed before the rain started again. It stopped after some minutes, but before we had got much further along the Track we were once again looking at the world through a veil of cold, wet water.

This exasperating rainfall pattern was repeated several times, which made walking particularly tedious, even though the actual distance was only a couple of kilometres longer than the previous day.

We arrived at Long Point, on a ridge overlooking the ocean, shortly after one in the afternoon, and for one very brief, insane moment we actually considered pushing on to Woolbales, another seventeen kilometres. We knew that we would have to double up at least once in order for Andris to arrive in Balingup in time to connect with his bus on the 16th April, and it was a matter of selecting two short-walking days that were back to back. To double up or, as many call it, to 'double hut' means to walk from campsite A to campsite C in one day, hopping over campsite B.

Thankfully, the moment of consideration did not last long. Apart from the fact that Andris was not very keen on the idea of doubling up, there was also the worry of it beginning to rain again and our getting really wet and having to camp halfway to Woolbales, all three of us in the one small tent. In spite of the negatives, Jonathan could still see certain advantages with pushing on, but very heavy rain set in about an hour after our arrival at Long Point, and it teemed, non-stop, all afternoon, all evening and all night.

Long Point shelter, in a beautiful, secluded position about five hundred metres off the Track, is rather lovely, but its main attraction for us was as a very welcome protection from the rain. Rob and Chris were still with us, having arrived at the shelter shortly before we did.

When we were filling in the campsite register, we were delighted to see that Gordon was still on the Track and that he was about a day ahead of us, most probably at Woolbales. We would have liked to have caught up with him, but we could not see how that was going to be possible.

Every shelter has a register that must be filled in by walkers doing any part of the Walk. The information – names and ages of walkers, how many, start point, proposed end point, intended next campsite and optional comment – can be vitally important, as Jonathan and I were to discover further along the Track.

Because of all the rain and the fact that we were all so wet and cold when we arrived at Long Point, we turned lunch into a cooked dinner, and later in the afternoon we had a second dinner. With no heating, hot showers or warm blankets, we were hoping that the warm food might go some way towards warding off the cold and the damp. Then, having hung all our wet clothes around the inside of the shelter, we spent the night listening to the rain pounding on the tin roof. It was actually so loud that it was impossible to hear the snorers snoring!

Day Thirteen
Thursday 31st March

Long Point to Woolbales

When we woke the next morning, it was to a vague awareness that it was the last day of March. In the early morning, the rain eased a fraction, and we all decided that the sky was actually looking a little lighter. As we packed up and made breakfast, we were hoping for a definite change in the weather. Much later, we heard that this particular week had broken all March records in Western Australia: the hottest March day, the coldest March day and the wettest March day. The 31st March was the day recorded as the wettest March day.

For about ten minutes, at the most, the walking was not all that bad: the rain was nowhere as heavy as it had been during the night, and it was fairly intermittent, so we were optimistic that it would soon stop altogether. After an initial ascent away from the campsite, we continued in a westerly direction with the Southern Ocean on our left. Unfortunately, the rain did not stop but became heavier the further we moved away from the camp.

After about an hour, we were all fairly wet and cold, and we were all feeling a little miserable: as far as we could see, there was no sign of the rain stopping or even easing. It became more and more obvious that the rain was not going anywhere soon, and Andris believed that the only thing to do was to abandon the Track and head for a nearby road. If we could get to one of the tracks leading to the South Western Highway, he had calculated that we could possibly pick up a lift to Northcliffe. He had looked at the map and knew that the Track crossed the Mandalay Beach Road just past Mandalay Beach.

A very rainy day

I was horrified: the Beach Road did not appear to be much more than a rough track, and there was absolutely no guarantee that we would be able to get a lift – who in their right mind would be out and about in such weather?

Even though I could understand his need to get out of the rain, I definitely did not feel that he, or anyone, should leave the Track. I was worried and quite uncertain as to what I should do: if I did nothing, and he ended up with hypothermia, I was certain that it would be completely my fault.

Like all of us, he was very cold, and his one thought was to alleviate the situation in whatever way he could. For me it was important that we stayed together, and if he insisted on leaving the Track then we would have no choice but to go with him. Even though the conditions were atrocious, it was indisputable that by following the Track we would eventually have to reach a shelter. If we turned away from the Track, anything could happen.

I was more than just slightly relieved when he finally decided that it made more sense to keep to the Track.

There were absolutely no animals to be seen anywhere, at least not living animals. I did see a dead baby marsupial of some kind, and some time later we all saw a large dead bird of prey; other than that there was nothing. I was hoping that the birds had all found somewhere to perch out of the rain and that they had not drowned.

Eventually, after about five or six kilometres, the Track again moved very close to the coast, and we began descending through some really awesome sand dunes to reach Mandalay Beach.

By now, the storm was in full swing, and the ocean – a confusion of greys and dark-toned purples verging on black – was covered with racing white horses. The sky was steely blue, and the sand had almost disappeared beneath the rough surf and the onslaught of the rain. It would have made a fantastic photo, but I had to keep the camera in the pack for fairly obvious reasons.

We stopped for a few minutes behind the toilet building near the beach, in the hope of getting some respite from the weather. When this proved impossible, we left the beach via a very long and steep staircase. At the top, we turned north and soon reached a ridge. Andris was now well ahead of me, and he took a wrong turn, which was not so difficult to do in the blinding rain. None of us noticed what he had done as visibility was restricted to only a few centimetres in all directions, but something must have made him question his choice of track. He quickly backtracked and fell in after Jonathan, who was some way behind me.

If it had not been teeming rain, this part of the Track, relatively level and straight, could have been really nice walking, but there was absolutely no protection anywhere from the constant heavy driving rain. We had no choice but to keep on walking whether we wanted to or not.

We were all completely drenched, from top to toe, and it was simply a matter of counting steps and pushing on. Initially our wet-weather gear attempted to put up a reasonable fight, but the water put up a bigger fight, easily finding a way inside all the protective layers of clothing, saturating us. The rain flattened our hair and then washed over our faces, making it difficult to focus on the Track. Thin streams of cold water ran down our necks. Our boots squelched at every step we took, and I began to get some idea of what a car must experience when being driven through a car wash. We were all clinging to that simple law of physics that assured us that by moving in a straight line from A to B we would eventually *have* to reach the shelter.

Cold, sopping wet and very subdued, we reached the Woolbales shelter around two in the afternoon. I had read that there are some amazing views from above the campsite, which is situated among the granite rocks of the Woolbale Hills; however, for some reason, no one was even vaguely interested in views.

As we unstrapped our packs and pulled ourselves, dripping wet, up on to the platform of the shelter, we saw that Gordon was still there, which was possibly *the* highlight of the day. We learnt that he had spent the whole day in the shelter, not wanting to venture any further in the rain. Rob and Chris, also very wet and cold, had arrived not long before we did.

We all spent the next couple of hours trying to dry everything: our clothes on improvised lines hung all around the hut and our boots the best way we could, during which time we made dinner and commiserated with each other. We were extremely grateful for the shelter: the air temperature was no more than fifteen degrees; it was still teeming rain and extremely windy; and it continued to pour relentlessly all night.

Day Fourteen
Friday 1st April

Woolbales to Mount Chance

I am not sure if the fact that it was April Fool's Day had anything to do with it, but we woke to yet another day of rain and low temperatures. Andris and I did not get away from Woolbales until almost ten, by which time Gordon, Chris and Rob had all left.

Getting back into our still wet, cold clothes was indescribably awful, especially knowing that we were facing the probability of yet another day of rain and cold. However, we had no choice. Also, we knew that we would have to complete the twenty-plus kilometres ahead of us without taking any breaks; there is really not much point stopping for a rest break in teeming rain.

The one thing that was positive was the terrain: it was quite flat. As with the previous day, the walking would have been quite easy had the weather been better. We spent the entire day within the boundaries of the Shannon National Park where, after about twelve or thirteen kilometres, we passed fairly close to Mount Pingerup (height 176 metres). There was the option of climbing to the summit; however, neither of us was particularly keen, and we kept walking. Between Mount Pingerup and Mount

Chance we crossed the Pingerup Plains (also flat), but because water always tends to find the path of least resistance flatness was no longer an advantage, and most of the Track was a raging stream. No matter how hard we tried to avoid the worst of the water, our boots were very soon soaked through. Again.

Jonathan left the shelter some time after we did, and he did not catch up to us as he normally would have done. Because of the cold and the miserable conditions, I was somewhat concerned, even though I knew that there was really no cause for worry and that he just needed to be on his own for a bit. As he said later, the walk the previous day, with the constant heavy rain and the biting cold, had left him feeling completely shattered; even after the night at Woolbales, he was still feeling fairly out of sorts – *depressed* was probably the better word – which meant that he had neither the energy nor the inclination to be particularly social.

Andris and I reached the shelter at Mount Chance around three-thirty in the afternoon, and Jonathan got in just before four. Needless to say, I was very relieved.

Gordon, however, had not arrived, and even as evening set in there was still no sign of him. When Andris and I turned up at Mount Chance, Chris and Rob and another fellow, Sasha, (who had started in Pemberton and was going south) had all claimed their parts of the shelter and were trying to warm themselves as best as they could. Chris and Rob had been hoping that Gordon might have been with us, and they were disappointed and concerned when they heard that we had no idea where he was. We all wondered whether he may have decided to continue on to Dog Pool, even though we knew that such a decision would have been insane, considering the weather. On the other hand, he may have taken a wrong turn, which would have been very easy to do given the weather, and there was a slight chance that he could have ended up on the highway. If this was what happened, I was sincerely hoping that he had been able to get a lift. Everyone, even Sasha, who had never met Gordon, was extremely concerned.

After hanging our drenched articles of clothing wherever we could in the shelter, we cooked dinner. Just before nightfall, Sasha took a torch and went up to the ridge behind the hut and signalled, in the unlikely event that if Gordon was lost somewhere near the campsite it might help him get his bearings.

We all felt very helpless, but there was really nothing more that we could do. For the entire duration of the night, the rain continued to pelt down.

Day Fifteen
Saturday 2nd April

Mount Chance to Dog Pool

It was difficult to fully comprehend when we woke up in the morning and dragged ourselves out of our sleeping bags, it was actually sunny. I felt as if we should have all been doing some kind of sun dance as a mark of gratitude. But while I was extremely thankful I was also very aware of the dangers of being overly optimistic: when we finally left the campsite, I made sure that I was wearing my wet-weather trousers with my jacket slung on the outside of my pack.

We set off with considerably raised spirits. Sasha (who was going in the opposite direction) had told us that it was a gradual descent all the way to Dog Pool, but this was his own experience, walking north to south, and it was actually a gradual ascent.

We left the campsite just before nine o'clock, and for the entire four hours it took us to reach the Dog Pool campsite, we were, like the previous day, walking through the Shannon National Park. Once again, it was quite flat, and the walking was easy, particularly with the sun shining and no sign of the dreadful rain that had plagued us for several days. In parts it was quite obvious that the sandy, coastal-type vegetation was beginning to give way to the forest vegetation more associated with the northern part of the Track.

Finally we crossed the footbridge over the Shannon River and saw the Dog Pool shelter ahead of us. In spite of having had several hours of really pleasant walking, we were still very happy to see the shelter; as we came closer, we were tremendously relieved to see Gordon sitting out in front, enjoying the sun.

He told us how he must have missed the sign to the Mount Chance campsite – a sign that was actually only a few metres from the shelter – and in the pouring rain he had unknowingly continued along the Track towards Dog Pool. He had walked a good six kilometres beyond Mount Chance before he understood what he had done, at which point he had sat down on the sodden ground and wept. He was far too tired to return to Mount Chance, but he also knew that there was no possibility of his reaching Dog Pool before dark. He had no tent, and it was unbelievably wet and cold. He moved into some bushes at the side of the Track, wrapped himself in a large, plastic garbage bag that he happened to have in his pack, took a sleeping tablet, and with the rain teeming around him and over him he spent one of the worst nights of his life, waiting for the dawn. In the morning, completely amazed that he had actually survived the night, he pushed on to Dog Pool.

Rob and Chris were already at the campsite and had a cheery fire going (this is the first campsite, going north, where fires are allowed). We strung up lines and soon all the contents of our packs were laid out in the sun or hung on lines, drying happily.

We all had a really pleasant evening around the fire and went to bed early, relieved that we now had dry clothes to put on in the morning.

Day Sixteen
Sunday 3rd April

Dog Pool to Lake Maringup

We woke to wonderful sunshine and birdsong, the birds having not drowned after all, and we were well on our way by eight. Although there is a gradual ascent after leaving the campsite, the almost twenty-five kilometres between Dog Pool and Maringup are, on the whole, very flat. The Track wends its way though swampy areas with paperbarks, stunted jarrah and tea tree. It dramatically changes direction several times, first west and then, after about six kilometres, south, before, around the eighteen kilometre mark, turning west again. The last couple of kilometres before the campsite are again due south.

About halfway to Maringup, we met up with a party of day walkers going in the opposite direction. The leader told me that he had done the whole Track two years previously and that the particular section where we now were walking had then been *so* wet that he had had water up to his waist for almost the entire day. Although there was a slight Monty Python ring to the story, I was able to believe him, especially after what we had just been through, and things immediately took on a completely different perspective. I began to wonder what it was that we had been complaining about.

All of the area between Dog Pool and Maringup falls within either the Shannon or the D'Entrecasteaux National Parks, and it is not only flat but also extremely swampy. As confirmation of what the man had told us, I have since heard that it is not uncommon for almost the entire Track to be under water, especially during the winter months. Then, but probably at any time of the year, there is certainly reason to be thankful for the many scattered islands of forest.

The walking was predominantly easy, as long as we were able to ignore the long, spindly grass, which spreads itself dangerously over the track, and on which I tripped more than once. Although the grass was a nuisance, we were so happy and thankful to have dry, sunny weather again, we would probably have put up with anything.

Once again, we were surrounded by lots of birds, and it was wonderful to know that they had not drowned. As well as being able to enjoy a return to birdsong, I was also pleased to be able to wear my sandals in order to give my feet a much-needed rest.

It was two-thirty when we arrived at the campsite, which is situated on the banks of the beautiful Lake Maringup, a large lake covering about 150 hectares. Only accessible by foot – the closest access point by road being eight kilometres to the east – the relative isolation of the lake means that not only has it created a haven for birds and wildlife, but it has also allowed the entire area to retain its natural and unchanged beauty.

This time, though, the hut was full. Besides the three of us and Gordon and Rob and Chris, there was a couple from Northcliffe and two men (also from Northcliffe), but, fortunately, we all managed to find somewhere to spread out our sleeping bags.

The three of us planned to get away early the next day, as we had already decided to double up to Northcliffe.

Day Seventeen
Monday 4th April

Maringup to Gardner to Northcliffe

With the doubling up, this was going to be a 31-kilometre day, so we made sure that we were up by five-thirty and well under way by six-thirty. Early on it was quite cool, but as the day became older it reached at least 28°C.

We were once again walking in a northerly direction, and the Track, like on the previous two or three days, was relatively flat. Even though the terrain was level, the ground itself, strewn with a mixture of leaves, small branches, roots and stones, was fairly uneven, which is not the very best surface for sandals, so I was once again wearing my boots.

After two or three kilometres, we reached the Gardner River, which we then kept company all the way to the Gardner River campsite. With the river within sight or hidden beyond the wall of trees lining the Track, we walked along sandy roads and trudged through areas that were most likely swampy at other times of the year; we also passed through a fair bit of karri forest.

Karri trees are quite impressive not only because of their height, but also because of the way mature trees only branch from the top third of the tree, making the massive trunk all the more prominent. The trunk can vary in colour between white, grey and brown, with white being the dominant colour, while the leaves are dark green on top and light-green underneath. From what I have read, the trees have cream-coloured flowers in the spring and summer, but when we were on the Track there were, of course, no flowering karri trees.

After following the river for some kilometres, and after negotiating a number of creek crossings, we reached Gardner at eleven in the morning. There was a sign on the rainwater tank telling us that there was some kind of problem with the water (it may have been that the level had dropped too low), and we were advised to take water from the river but to treat it properly before drinking. Fortunately, we still had sufficient water to get us to Northcliffe, so we did not bother about filtering river water. Being able to use rainwater from the campsite tanks for practically all of the Walk meant that we rarely had to treat the water; however, we did have a water filter with us, and we did use it on several occasions.

I rested for about twenty minutes and then set off on my own along the Track towards Northcliffe. Andris and Jonathan stayed at Gardner somewhat longer.

Once again we had lost Gordon. He had left Maringup before us, also intending to do the double up, but he was not at Gardner when we arrived, and we had not seen any sign of him on the Track.

He arrived at Gardner just as Andris and Jonathan were thinking of leaving, and he told them how he had managed to take a wrong turn that had added several unnecessary kilometres to his walk. By the time he reached Gardner, he was fairly tired, and he decided not to double up. He said that he would remain at the campsite overnight and continue on to Northcliffe the following day.

That was the very last time any of us saw Gordon.

Much later, after we had finished the Walk and had returned to the east coast, I received a letter from Gordon, who was then back in Albany. In the letter, he told me that he had run out of water before he reached Gardner, and that (as we already knew) the tank water at the Gardner campsite was undrinkable. The first time he took water from the river, he used his water-treatment tablets; the following day, before continuing on to Northcliffe, he hastily collected some more water without treating it. As he wrote, it looked and tasted quite okay. His assessment turned out to be far from correct, and by the time he had reached Northcliffe he was not at all well, suffering as he was with stomach pains and general discomfort. He checked into the hotel and remained there for three days with dreadful diarrhoea. At the end of the three days, he decided that there was no point continuing with the Walk, and he took the bus back to Albany. As soon as he arrived home, some friends, realizing that he was much sicker than he was letting on, took him straight to Emergency. At the hospital, they discovered that not only was he completely dehydrated, but he was still suffering the consequences of having collided with some very nasty bug. He was placed on antibiotics and kept in hospital for four days.

Although the second lap, stretching from Gardner to

Northcliffe (just a little over fifteen kilometres), is also reasonably flat with only a very slight ascent towards Northcliffe, we all felt that the walking was distinctly more difficult than from Maringup to Gardner. This was probably because, by that stage of the day, we were all quite tired; in fact, by late afternoon, we were totally exhausted.

When we finally turned on to a disused railway track, close by a functioning sawmill, and checked the map, we were relieved to see that there was not much more than a kilometre left and that Northcliffe was more or less within a giant's stone's throw.

We finally reached Northcliffe around five in the afternoon. It is a small town, with approximately four hundred inhabitants, most of them involved with either farming or logging, the town itself being surrounded by jarrah, karri and marri forests.

Marri, like jarrah and karri, is also a type of eucalyptus, found only in the south-west of Western Australia. It has rough brown bark, can grow to 40 metres and has white flowers in summer; it also produces gumnuts or, as they are called in Western Australia, honkey nuts. Whether it is true or not, I have heard that the name *honkey* is a corruption of the word *hockey*, the nuts having been used in some variation of that particular game. The name *marri* comes from the Noongar word for blood and refers to the blood-like excretions of red gum from the trunk.

Besides the hotel where we stayed, a motel, a general store and a post office, there is really not very much in Northcliffe. The remaining buildings (mostly closed and boarded up) were all for sale by Ray White. There was also a roadhouse with an adjoining caravan park, where Jonathan took the washing. The woman at the hotel had told us that it was 'just down the road'; as it turned out, 'just down the road' was a euphemism for *a good two kilometres*.

While I was checking us in at the hotel, the television was on, and the news flashing across the screen was all about the current Pope, John Paul II, who had evidently died. If I was taken aback, it was not necessarily because of the news as such, but more because of a realization that during the time we had been in sublime isolation the world outside of the Track had been continuing with all its tragedy and intrigue. Things had not stopped simply because we were no longer paying any attention to them; the world and we were simply moving on two different tangents.

The hotel had a somewhat faded old-world feel about it – the dining room was actually called the *1945 Lounge* – and there were cheap prints by Monet and van Gogh adorning the walls of most of the corridors and rooms. The taps in the bathroom were brass and old-fashioned (one hot and one cold). There were small cracks here and there and fittings that did not fit properly, but there was a shower with wonderful hot water and soft, fluffy white towels, which more than made up for everything else. The people were extremely friendly, and we definitely enjoyed our short stay at the Northcliffe hotel.

After we had deposited all our things in the hotel room, Jonathan took the first lot of washing to the caravan park, and I followed a short time later with the second load. He remained there, taking care of the washing and drying, while he read his book until it became too dark for him to see the words on the page. When he finally got back with the clean, dry clothes, he showered, and later we had dinner (veggie burgers, chips and steamed vegetables) in the *1945 Lounge,* a fitting conclusion to a very long, and fairly arduous, day.

628 kms to Kalamunda

Section Two

Northcliffe to Balingup

The second section of the Bibbulmun Track, Northcliffe to Balingup, is roughly two hundred and fourteen kilometres in length. For a crow, the distance between the two places would be just over ninety kilometres, while a car following the main road would clock up about one hundred and twenty kilometres.

By Northcliffe, the Track has actually already turned away from the coast and has begun to move northwards on the long vertical stretch towards Kalamunda. Between Northcliffe and Balingup, the Track passes through large areas of forest (where the karri is most definitely the predominant tree) and also crosses many valleys, which must indicate the presence of just as many, or even more, hills.

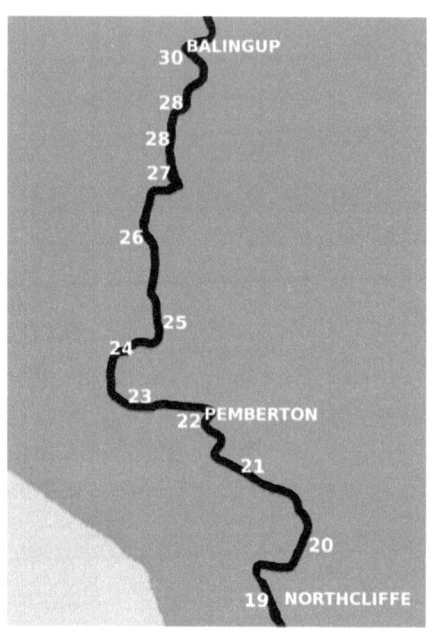

Northcliffe to Balingup 215 kilometres

19 *Northcliffe*
20 Schafer
21 Warren
22 *Pemberton*
23 Beedelup
24 Beavis
25 Boarding House
26 Tom Road
27 *Donnelly River Village*
28 Gregory Brook
29 Blackwood
30 *Balingup*

(Italics indicate hotel or backpacker accommodation).

Day Eighteen
Tuesday 5th April

Northcliffe to Schafer

There would be no more doubling up until after Andris left us in Balingup. Although he had now fully recovered from the rather debilitating virus he had picked up before the beginning of the Walk, he was still not keen on doing overly long days of walking. It was a relief to know that the doubling up we had already done meant that, even doing just one campsite a day, we would reach Balingup in time for Andris to connect with his bus and, ultimately, his flight back to Sydney.

After a breakfast of cereal, toast, coffee and chocolate in the little kitchen upstairs, we visited the post office where Jonathan and I both posted parcels home: I was getting rid of a few more things deemed unnecessary, and Jonathan was posting his book. The book, *Shantaram* by Gregory David Roberts, which Jonathan finished reading the previous evening, weighed close to one kilo, so I can understand that he was probably extremely relieved that he no longer had to carry it. From a weight perspective, it was certainly not the type of book one would normally recommend taking on a long Walk.

We then went to the general store and bought supplies. By the time we had everything sorted and packed, it was already ten, and we hoisted our packs on to our backs and headed for Schafer.

Although the morning had dawned reasonably cool and very misty, by the time we finally left Northcliffe, the sun had come out, the mist had lifted and it was obvious that it was going to be a beautiful day.

Andris

Not far out of Northcliffe, we passed a sign telling us that it was 335 kilometres to Albany and 628 kilometres to Kalamunda; a small reminder that, even after seventeen days, we still had a long way to go to reach the halfway mark. From our calculations, the halfway point was somewhere near Donnelly River Village, almost one hundred and fifty kilometres further along the Track.

For about a kilometre we walked in an easterly direction mainly through forest, but then the Track gradually swung around towards the north, and by the time we had walked a further four or five kilometres, through forest and alongside farmland, we were walking directly north. There were also several sections of road walking, and most of the time there was a very slight ascent (after all, we *were* going north).

On an open, sandy flat, we saw, without the slightest exaggeration, *thousands* of grasshoppers. We also saw a little grey-white bunny, and I assume that he probably had many friends and relatives that we could not see. We failed to notice any snakes, though rustling sounds in the grass made us think of them, with good reason. There were lots of magpies, with their beautiful warbling, and for the first time on the Track we saw blackberry bushes. Somewhere around the eleven-kilometre mark, the Track moved away from the farming land and back into forest.

We arrived at the empty campsite at Schafer, fourteen kilometres north of Northcliffe, around two-thirty in the afternoon. The campsite is named after Geoff Schafer, who first had the idea for the Track in the early 1970s. His dream was eventually realized in 1979, when the Track was opened; twenty years later, a new alignment (which was the one we were walking) replaced Schafer's Track, retaining less than ten percent of the original alignment.

The new Track came about thanks to Jesse Brampton. In the late 1980s, he walked the Appalachian Trail in USA, a track that extends for more than 3,000 kilometres between Georgia and Maine. On his return to Australia,

Brampton then walked the Bibbulmun Track. He was shocked by the comparison between the two Tracks: much of the Bibbulmun Track was on gravel roads, there were no shelters, the water sources were unreliable and the signage was less than satisfactory. Joining together with other walkers who felt that there was a lot that could be done with the Track, he drew up a proposal for improvements which included, among other things: a realignment, shelters, toilets, rainwater tanks and more signs. This proposal was accepted by the Department of Conservation and Land Management (CALM), who then set to work to turn the Bibbulmun Track into one of the world's great long-distance walking tracks.

Schafer is a glorious spot, and the shelter looks out over a beautiful dam, most of which is on private property. As it was still very sunny when we arrived, Jonathan went for a swim, but both Andris and I decided that the water looked far too cold. After his swim and after drying off, Jonathan built up the fire; the fire, more or less, having become Jonathan's responsibility. It was something he enjoyed, and whether or not it had anything to do with him being born under a fire sign is difficult to say.

While we were cooking dinner, a well-dressed lady with a pram came along the Track. It was a very surreal image: a demure, beautifully dressed lady pushing a pram through what could only be described as the wilderness. She told us that she lived on a nearby farm and that she usually liked to take a walk around the dam of an evening. She was quite charming and stayed and talked for a while. After dinner, which took some time to cook, we went to bed. As we lay snuggled up in our sleeping bags, we could hear a cow lowing in the distance.

Day Nineteen
Wednesday 6th April

Schafer to Warren

With a 21-kilometre day ahead of us, we were already up by five-thirty. It was still dark, but the cow had started lowing again, and some ducks nearby were engaged in either a confrontation or a very noisy conversation; it was difficult to say which.

By the time we left Schafer an hour later, it was light but still quite misty. The Track skirted the dam for a short way and then turned into the forest. Not long after entering the forest, we came across a STINKING pile of dead black cow right in the middle of the Track. From a distance we thought that it may have been one of the many burnt logs we had seen, but it did not take us long to ascertain what it actually was. We made an impromptu detour from the actual Track to bypass the poor animal that could actually no longer be called an animal, and rejoined the Track a little further on.

The first part of the day's walk was mainly on a descending Track, and the few very small hills we met were of very little consequence; in fact, they completely paled in comparison with one of the extreme hazards of forest walking: the gumnuts from the marri trees.

As I mentioned earlier, gumnuts, or honkey nuts, are the fruit of the marri. The nuts are round, very hard and extremely prolific; wherever the marri is growing, the nuts can be found absolutely everywhere on the ground. As could be expected, they are extremely treacherous: unwary feet easily roll on them as they would on any kind of small, hard, round ball. The nuts, more than bark, sticks and fallen trees, make the ground underfoot just so much more difficult to navigate.

We heard many magpies and saw more and more blackberry bushes. Over the years, the bushes have encroached on agricultural and pastoral areas, as well as blocking many creeks and creating fire hazards. On top of all of this, their thorny branches provide a protective haven for snakes. The fact that they produce delicious, small, black berries tends to pale alongside all the negatives, and the blackberry is now classified as a Weed of National Significance throughout all of Australia.

After about ten kilometres, we crossed McAlpine Road, which is a major log-hauling road, and not long afterwards we met up with the Warren River. The rather dense vegetation meant that we only got scattered glimpses of the river, but most of the time we knew that it was there. The closer we came to Warren campsite, the hillier became the terrain, which forced us to take a number of short rest breaks. We crossed several bridges, including one with long extensions at each end (evidently the creek swells when it rains) and which, for whatever reason, turned out to be a delightfully bouncy bridge.

The forests were beautiful. There were lots of karri trees, but also a type of pale-green tree, the name of which we did not know. Eventually, we crossed the Warren River on the Warren River Bridge, a very long footbridge (155 metres), and almost immediately climbed an unbelievably awful hill that just kept going up and up and up at an absurdly steep angle. I was extremely grateful when, at around one-thirty, we reached the campsite.

The Track had been completely ours all day (except for a brief meeting with a party of three walking from Pemberton to Schafer), and now even Warren campsite was completely ours. We unstrapped our packs and lay on the floor of the shelter, soaking up the sleepy warmth of the afternoon sun.

Day Twenty
Thursday 7th April

Warren to Pemberton

When we crawled out of our sleeping bags and pulled on our clothes, it was just past five in the morning. It was still dark, but by the time we left the campsite an hour later the sun was well and truly on its way up. Jonathan wanted to have a day on his own, so he went on ahead and reached Pemberton some time before eleven.

Although the day eventually turned out to be quite warm, the early start meant that for the first part of the day's walking it was still relatively cool; it was also very misty. On the whole, even though the Track seemed somewhat tangled at times, and there were a number of hills, the walking was quite pleasant. We crossed several vehicle tracks and logging roads before, after about thirteen kilometres, reaching the diversion track to the Cascades. We decided against diverting to look at the Cascades themselves (even though I had heard that they are quite beautiful), took a short break and then trudged up the final hill to the Gloucester Tree. I had actually entertained ideas about climbing the tree until I saw it, when I very quickly changed my mind.

In the 1940s, fire lookouts were built in a number of karri trees throughout the forest, and the Gloucester Tree is one of these. The tree was named after His Royal Highness the Duke of Gloucester, the then Governor-General of Australia, who just happened to be visiting Pemberton when the lookout was being built. It is more than sixty metres in height, and metal rungs have been placed around the trunk providing both footholds and handholds. Although it is said that the view from the top is stupendous, the height of the tree made me decide that it was really not worth the effort. I later found out that Jonathan, who is not quite as earthbound as I am, did actually climb the tree. He agreed with the general opinion: the view *is* stupendous.

Andris and I finally reached Pemberton a good two hours after Jonathan. The place, once called *Wandergarup* 'place of much water' by the local Aboriginal people, is a timber town and has been involved with timber since long before the 1920s when it first received the name of Pemberton. Over recent years the focus of the timber industry has moved from old-growth forest timber to plantation timber, and now there is also an emphasis on tourism and wine production.

We had pre-booked at the Pemberton Backpackers, so we made our way to Brockman Street where we met Keith, the man in charge. He seemed pleasant and showed us the little cottage where we would be staying. While we were unpacking and working out what needed to be washed and what we needed to buy in the way of supplies, Jonathan, who had been out shopping, arrived with lemonade and potato chips.

Later, during the afternoon, we did our shopping, I organized the washing and then I borrowed the Internet at the Backpackers. Finally, we had dinner at the Shamrock Café, which was located across the road from the backpackers.

The place itself was reasonably pleasant, but the waitress was a complete disappointment. When we asked if it was possible to order potatoes and vegetables, she responded brusquely, "How long do you think you want to wait?"

Deciding that potatoes and vegetables had been relegated to the too-hard basket, Jonathan and I ordered spinach turnovers, and Andris had spring rolls; we then had apple and berry pie, which was a slightly decadent change from the very basic food we had been used to on the Track. Because of the very long wait between courses (which made absolutely no sense given that all the food came out of the freezer), the whole meal took an unbelievable two hours.

After dinner, we got our packs ready for the next morning and then went to bed to the sound of the sawmill across the road, a sound that continued until at least ten in the evening.

Crossing a swing bridge

Day Twenty-One
Friday 8th April

Pemberton to Beedelup

We were woken by a rooster doing his very best to crow, which was a slight disappointment after all the birdsong on the Track, but it was still much better than many other options. Also, the sawmill had started up again, so we were out of bed reasonably early. After eating breakfast, Andris and I left Pemberton before eight o'clock, with Jonathan following a short while afterwards.

The Track, running more or less in a northerly direction, passed through a park and alongside the public swimming baths, which for some unknown reason, were not actually used for swimming, before starting to ascend through mixed forest, where we saw a dead rabbit in the middle of the Track.

Had we been at all superstitious, we may have interpreted the dead animal as a prelude to something negative; however, given the large number of dead animals we had already passed on the Track, life would have been looking fairly bleak if the animals were in any way an indication of our fortunes. In spite of the rabbit, it turned out to be a very pleasant, sunny day, and the walking was relatively easy.

We accomplished the first five or six kilometres in record time and reached Big Brook Dam where we saw some rather shy black swans that did not want to be photographed. We also met a lady with two Scottish terriers, both of them sporting tartan collars. From Big Brook Dam, the Track then made a definite swing towards the west.

About three kilometres beyond the dam, we passed a small picnic area before entering the Big Brook Arboretum where there were many different kinds of trees, all of them displaying neat information labels. Beyond the arboretum, for the next nine or so kilometres, the walking, through mixed forest, was fairly uneventful, and we were, no doubt, lulled into a false sense of how wonderful things could be. Just before eleven-thirty and about two kilometres before Channybearup Road, it suddenly began to rain.

To begin with, the rain was not too heavy, and we knew that we would soon be entering the Beedelup National Park, where we were expecting that there would be a greater degree of cover. As a result, we were not overly worried; however, the closer we came to the park, the heavier the rain, and very soon everything we were wearing had become drenched. Clambering into rain clothes at that stage was definitely a case of shutting the stable door after the horse has bolted: the damage had, unfortunately, already been done.

Just as we were about to cross one of those rather ghastly but necessary stiles, with the rain still pelting down, Jonathan caught up with us. From that point, with more than three and a half kilometres remaining to the shelter, I was completely sure, at every turn of the Track, that I would see the roof of the shelter beckoning to us through the trees. I did not give up hope, even though three and a half kilometres is an awfully long way in teeming rain. When we finally rounded a bend in the

Track to see the shelter in front of us, my gratitude knew no bounds.

The shelter and campsite suddenly appearing from behind trees or over a hill or around a bend in the road is always a wonderful sight, and more so when the weather has been really bad or at the end of a long day of hard walking. The reality of the building means the end of the day's walking; it is the physicality of the words *to arrive*.

Once again we were all soaking wet, and, although it would have been comforting to have had a fire, getting anything to burn was out of the question: everything was completely sodden. We pulled out our little stove and made warm drinks; a bit later on, we heated up some bean mix and had tacos with filling.

Beedelup is believed to have come from a Noongar word, *Beejalup* 'a place of rest or a place of sleep', which we all agreed was a very appropriate name for a campsite. Then, just as we were about to zip ourselves into our sleeping bags, we heard a four-wheel drive vehicle pulling up outside the hut. Not being at all used to hearing vehicles near the campsites, the sound and what it might possibly mean was more than a little worrying. Images from scary horror films ran through my head, while Jonathan stepped outside the shelter to see what was going on.

He found two men from CALM sitting in the vehicle, the engine still turning over, and the windscreen wipers making that unique, monotonous, windscreen-wiper sound. One of the men rolled down his side window and said that they had been in the area, checking shelters and campsites, and, given the dreadful night, they were now looking for somewhere where they could camp with their crate of beer. Jonathan said that they were welcome to stay, but the man knew that we probably wanted to sleep, and sleep was not exactly what they had had in mind, so he shook his head, and, having rolled up the window, very decently moved on.

The rain continued teeming for some time; even when it eventually stopped, heavy drops of water kept falling noisily on to the roof from the trees above. During the night the temperature dropped to less than eight degrees, and for whatever reason I did not sleep very well.

Inside one of the southern huts

Day Twenty-Two
Saturday 9th April

Beedelup to Beavis

Because our clothes were still cold and wet from the previous day, it took us much longer to get dressed and moving in the morning, and we did not get away from the shelter until after nine. Try to imagine what it can feel like on a really cold, misty morning, stepping into still-not-dry trousers and pulling a damp, cold T-shirt over your head. If you are lucky, you may have a pair of dry, but not awfully clean, socks somewhere in the bottom of your pack, which you put on before thrusting your feet into no-longer-sopping-but-still-damp boots.

Fortunately, by the time we left, the sun had begun to shine, and we chose to look on it as a good omen. Andris and I left the shelter first, and we soon reached Beedelup Falls, which is a popular tourist spot. After looking at the Falls, we crossed below them on a very long suspension bridge. As I have already noted, I am not very brave with heights, and suspension bridges, particularly ones that sway from side to side as you walk across them, do not belong to my most favourite things; however, holding firmly – *firmly* is probably an understatement – on to the railings on each side of the bridge, I managed to reach the other side without any mishap.

We very soon left the Beedelup National Park, and entered a forest-logging area. By this time, Jonathan had caught up with us, and the three of us continued walking, mainly in a northerly direction, through a mixed jarrah and marri forest.

We crossed Carey Brook on a small footbridge and, further on, crossed a number of smaller creeks. The walking, most of it through the forest, was uneventful, though we did pass a couple of dead kangaroos, and we spent a fair bit of time trying to avoid gumnuts. About five kilometres before Beavis, we descended on to a gravel road and crossed the Donnelly River. From the river onwards, it was relatively hilly, especially the last bit before the campsite.

Then, just before eleven-thirty, it started to rain. Again.

We had to get back into our very wet wet-weather gear and cover our packs. The weather alternated frustratingly between rain and sunshine, so we were not sure whether to discard our wet-weather gear or not. Even though it was not heavy rain, we still managed to get quite wet.

We arrived at Beavis just after three in the afternoon and were met by an intangible, but very definite, feeling of negativity. I noticed that there was a swimming hole without water, but I knew that an empty water hole was not sufficient to cause such a gloomy, depressed feeling. While I was trying to put my finger on what might have been causing the strange feeling, I decided that I would have a turn at starting the fire; however, when I tried, it did not go quite the way I had imagined. Jonathan offered to give me a hand, but, just as he was about to do so, we noticed someone arriving from the north. The fire was momentarily forgotten as we watched the newcomer walking along the Track towards the campsite.

He was gnarled and wiry and, as we later learnt, seventy-three years old; he was wearing a green fabric hat, and, on his back, he had a small pack, which we soon discovered was full of canned food. He looked for all the world like a little forest gnome as he made his way towards the campsite, hugging an enormous roll of sleeping mat and a carton of eggs (most of which had already smashed when he had taken a fall). Like Gordon, he was from Albany.

Once he had reached the shelter and had lined up all his different packages on the table, he introduced himself as Eddie; he then told us that he had completed part of the Track some years previously. This time, he had started at Donnelly River and was aiming to get as far as Walpole.

In spite of his unorthodox approach to packs and packing, he definitely knew something about lighting fires, and very soon he and Jonathan had the fire burning, and we were able to start making our dinner and drying our clothes. After we had all finished preparing and eating dinner, we stood around the fire, keeping an eye on our bits and pieces of clothing while talking about the Track and fires and life in general.

It was a very clear night, and, as with most nights on the Walk, the stars were absolutely amazing. Standing in the middle of the bush, surrounded by a darkness that was only broken by the glow of the fire, it was difficult not be overwhelmed by the millions upon millions of small lights above us. Perhaps some of those tiny pinpricks of light are actually home to other forms of life, or perhaps there is nothing else out there but an endless space filled with luminous balls of gas. Whatever the case, it really makes no difference: the experience from the ground, somewhere along the Bibbulmun Track, would still have to be the same.

Because we really needed to get our clothes dried, we did not creep into our sleeping bags until some time after nine. Later, during the night, the temperature dropped several degrees below 10°C.

In spite of the wonderful night sky and the fire, and even in spite of Eddie, the negative feeling remained, and all three of us decided that Beavis was actually a very depressing place.

Day Twenty-Three
Sunday 10th April

Beavis to Boarding House

Thankfully, when we woke up in the morning, it was no longer raining. We said our goodbyes to Eddie, secretly hoping that he would manage with all his many bits and pieces, and we left the shelter well before eight.

After leaving the campsite and crossing a small creek, the Track kept quite close to the Donnelly River, winding for some kilometres north, before turning east through a really beautiful forest of karri and banksia.

Banksia, which is only found in Australia, was named after the botanist Sir Joseph Banks. There are many different varieties of banksia, and they range from ground cover to almost 30 metres in height. The actual flower spikes are made up of hundreds, or even thousands, of small flowers, and colours range from the palest of yellows to bright red. Many birds and small mammals feed on both the nectar and the old flower spikes.

Eventually the Track turned away from the river and began to move in a more northerly direction with a lot of ascending and descending; in fact, although the day's walk was not much more than nineteen kilometres, it turned out to be one of the more challenging days because of all the hills.

At one stage, while we were negotiating one of the steeper hills, some heavy black clouds appeared overhead. By now we had learnt to equate all black clouds with drenching rain, and I prayed fervently that we might be proven wrong this time. I felt that we definitely had endured sufficient rain to last, if not a lifetime, at least until the end of the Walk.

My prayers were miraculously answered, and after ten rain-free kilometres we stopped at Lease Road and took a short break. The final kilometres of the Track towards Boarding House were along a logging road, and we arrived at the empty shelter at two-thirty in the afternoon. After we had eaten and cleaned up, it actually did begin to rain, but with a roof over our heads we could enjoy the feeling of being on the inside looking out. During the night, the temperature, once again, dropped well below 10°C.

Day Twenty-Four
Monday 11th April

Boarding House to Tom Road

We left Boarding House just before eight o'clock. The sun was shining, there was lots of birdsong, and the Track, compared with the previous day, was both easy and enjoyable. It was not raining, and everyone was feeling much more positive.

Shortly after leaving the campsite, we crossed the Donnelly River on the Boarding House Bridge, which is a footbridge built by the Army Reserve Field Engineers from a single fallen karri tree.

During the first few kilometres, the Track, which was still moving in a northerly direction, crossed a number of small creeks, and for the entire day it kept very close to the river.

About halfway to Tom Road, we arrived at One Tree Bridge in the One Tree Bridge Conservation Park. In the guide book, we had read that there was a café close to the bridge, and the three of us were all looking forward to being able to drink coffee there. In fact, for the final kilometre before the café, each of us had been thinking about what we were about to enjoy; consequently, our disappointment was quite profound when we saw that the café was closed because it was Monday. There was really not much we could do about it, not even frustrated banging on the door was going to change the situation. Still dreaming of cups of steaming hot coffee and wickedly seductive cakes, we had a short rest and then continued on our way.

One Tree Bridge received its name after an enormous karri tree was felled in 1904 to create a crossing over the 25-metre wide Donnelly River. Although there are similarities between this bridge and the Boarding House Bridge, both having been constructed from a single karri tree, the One Tree Bridge was capable of bearing both the weight and the breadth of bullock teams, while the Boarding House Bridge is a single-file footbridge.

In 1904 a graphite mine opened near the Donnelly River. That the graphite turned out to be of inferior quality is beside the point, the existence of the mine, and its possible future development, plus the need to be able to transport timber and people across the river, meant that a reliable crossing was necessary.

The One Tree Bridge came into being when two axe men located a suitable karri tree on one of the banks of the river. They then cleverly chopped the tree in such a way that it fell perfectly into position across the river. A superstructure, built from jarrah, was placed on top of the tree, and the resulting bridge was actually wide enough and strong enough to allow bullock teams to cross the river.

A bush fire in 1933 damaged the bridge, which was later repaired, but by the early 1940s it was declared too dangerous for general use, and it was closed. A new bridge was built a few years later, and the old One Tree Bridge eventually rotted away. Finally, after a wild storm sometime in the 1960s, the bridge fell into the river. The story does, however, have a reasonably happy ending, as part of the original bridge was retrieved from the river in the early 1970s and was rebuilt on the western bank as a monument both to the inventiveness of the men who built the original bridge and to the amazing strength and durability of the karri tree.

The poet Adam Lindsay Gordon, whose best-known collection of poems, *Bush Ballads and Galloping Rhymes,* was published just before he committed suicide in 1870, once owned land on the eastern side of the Donnelly River, more or less where the One Tree Bridge would later be constructed. He arrived in the area in 1866 as one of the very first settlers in the area. Later, having bought land and built a cottage, he leased an extra 20,000 hectares and attempted to run sheep. The country was not sheep-friendly, and, after a couple of years and many losses, he was forced to pack up and leave. Unfortunately, the many poems Adam wrote during this period were destroyed.

The area through which we were walking was reasonably hilly but still thickly forested, and the Track continued close to the Donnelly River all the way to Tom Road. Eventually, after walking through a forest of very tall trees and crossing two bridges, we descended to the campsite. Our arrival was greeted not only by a wallaby but also by a man and his three grandchildren: the man and the children were on the point of leaving, the wallaby was obviously staying.

Later, after we had settled ourselves into the shelter, a couple in their thirties arrived. They had been driven along Tom Road to within 150 metres of the campsite, and they both looked especially clean and fresh. After we had all introduced ourselves, they told us that they were intending to walk for two weeks, resting up for a day or so at several different campsites along the Track.

By seven-thirty we were all in our sleeping bags, and I believe that our wallaby kept guard outside the shelter for most of the night.

Day Twenty-Five
Tuesday 12th April

Tom Road to Donnelly River

Yet again we woke to birdsong. It was not raining, but a thin veil of grey mist had wrapped itself around the trees, giving an unreal appearance to the world beyond the walls of the shelter. Our wallaby had evidently decided that he was off duty and had possibly disappeared somewhere to enjoy a well-deserved rest because he was nowhere to be seen.

We were ready to leave at 7.45, by which time the other two people in the shelter were up and had begun to build the fire for their breakfast.

The beginning of the day's walk was fairly hilly, but later the terrain flattened out, and the walking became extremely pleasant. The mist lifted, leaving us with a crisp, cold day. It was shortly after the mist disappeared that we became aware of rather strange warm puffs of wind that smelt very strongly of ozone; then, without very much warning, it clouded over. By ten in the morning, it was definitely beginning to look like rain.

We had already walked more than eleven kilometres, so we took a break, and we put the covers on our packs. A short time later, our fears were actually realized, and it *did* start to rain. On the plus side, it was a soft, gentle kind of rain, but it was still wet, and it kept up for the entire hour it took for us to reach Donnelly River Village.

Donnelly River was named by Governor Stirling after a friend of his wife's family, Admiral Ross Donnelly. Although timber milling in the area began as early as 1912, activity ground to a halt only two years later, and it was not until the late 1940s that the original plans for the area were resurrected. A steam-driven mill was then installed, cottages were built for workers and the area flourished as a mill town for the best part of thirty years. Some years after the mill was deemed inefficient, the village, in the middle of a karri forest, was heritage listed and turned into a holiday village. The workers' cottages became accommodation for tourists, and the school was converted into a bunking place for hikers doing the Bibbulmun Track. The general store is now a café (with basic essentials, especially for walkers doing the Track), while the butcher's shop is a place where children can watch films. The original steam-driven mill is still part of the landscape, and the dozens of very tame kangaroos, emus, possums and even birds that frequent the area are a major attraction.

After a not-so-healthy snack of lemonade and chips from the general store, we walked over to the old school, where we found accommodation – a room with two bunk beds and access to a kitchen and bathroom – for $15.00 per person. We were also very pleased to discover that the general store had a couple of washing machines and a dryer that we could use for a small fee. We filled one of the washing machines, had showers with unbelievably wonderful hot water and then returned to the store for lunch.

After lunch, we bought a few supplies, I posted my postcards, and Jonathan borrowed the Internet in the shop.

The sun finally came out, chasing away the rain, and we took a short walk around the village, where we were amazed by the large number of kangaroos and emus who were either strutting around the place or lazily lying in the shade. The abundant, tame animal life, together with the large number of families with children, gave the place a definite holiday atmosphere, and it was actually a pleasant break from the Track. However, although we were enjoying the temporary break from our normal routine, we were also keeping our fingers firmly crossed that the sun would remain and that we would have good weather the following day.

Around four in the afternoon, Peter and Jeanette from America arrived. They were walking the Track in a north-south direction, and as walkers, they were also allotted bunks in the school building. After dinner, we all sat and talked for a while. As well as recounting some of their experiences so far on the Track, Peter and Jeanette were able to give us some advice concerning the northern part of the Track, while we, in turn, gave our impression of the southern part.

Day Twenty-Six
Wednesday 13th April

Donnelly River to Gregory Brook

Andris was almost at the end of his part of the Walk. It had all gone ever so much more quickly than I had imagined it would, and it felt strange to think that he would be leaving us in Balingup in only three days' time.

The morning of Wednesday the 13th April was really beautiful: it was sunny and reasonably warm, and it looked as though the rain might have finally left us. All our finger-crossing and praying had obviously been answered. After packing our things together and eating breakfast, we left the village just before eight, with the many kangaroos and emus clearly eager to see us off and say goodbye.

From the moment we left Donnelly River, this was an easy-walking day. At the outskirts of the village, we passed the old timber mill and, almost immediately, turned on to Snake Road, a gravel road that parallels the river. We walked through amazing forests as they shifted between karri, jarrah and blackbutt. Blackbutt (or yarri as it is also called) is a type of eucalyptus; it can grow to 50 metres, but the average height is around 20-30 metres, and, while the bark on the lower part of the tree is very rough, the bark higher up is quite smooth. The name *blackbutt* is a reference to the base of the tree, which is often completely black as the result of bush fire activity. The trees are supposed to be favoured by koalas, but, although we kept a diligent lookout, we did not see any of the fluffy, grey marsupials.

We did, however, see many kangaroos and lots of black-and-red cockatoos.

The Track, winding through forest and over a multitude of creeks and waterways, was extremely beautiful. At the Brockman Highway, towards the end of the day's walk, I went on ahead. Being completely alone (especially, or more importantly, when you know where you are), while surrounded by such beauty, solitude and quietness, is something very special.

It is not just the surrounding visual enchantment that is so enthralling; the unbelievable mixture of smells can often be quite extraordinary. There are the tree and plant smells, fresh, musty, heady and even narcotic, as well as the smells of bark mixed with the earthy tang of leaf matter. On hot days, all these smells are overlaid with the almost tangible aroma of heat; on rainy days, the smells compete with the clean, fresh scent of water.

Smells are so completely entwined with the visual experience of the Walk that the photos we took remind me not only of specific places along the Track but also of the fragrances and scents associated with just those particular places.

Any Walk is a wonderful opportunity for thinking about things or simply meditating; this Walk was no exception. Beyond all the challenges posed by the weather and the actual Track, there were actually no real distractions, and it became easier to focus on things that would normally be splintered by the many different kinds of auditory and visual discord that we are all subjected to on a daily basis. We usually chose to walk in our own space, treasuring the silence that, after all, is one of the reasons for the Walk in the first place. We saved most of our conversation for the breaks we had along the Track and for the campsites.

This Walk was no different to other long walks we had done, inasmuch as hours of constant walking, with no other distractions, meant that there was lots of time for thinking. Thoughts came and went; some of them returned in different forms, building on still other thoughts, creating platforms for new projects, new directions and even new experiences. There were also thoughts that concerned things that were problematic, many of them benefiting from the perspective and the focus that a long, uninterrupted Walk is able to provide.

Sometimes, when the walking was really difficult, the thoughts could be completely banal or without any meaning; they were simply a method of keeping the mind focused on something other than the four or five or ten kilometres that still had to be negotiated.

After about four kilometres, there was a gorgeous descent through the forest to the Gregory Brook shelter, where I arrived at one in the afternoon shortly before the other two.

That evening, the night sky was, as always, layered back to infinity with millions of stars, and it was both incredible and extremely humbling, but the lack of cloud meant that we knew that we could expect yet another very cold night. We were not wrong: it was freezing.

Day Twenty-Seven
Thursday 14th April

Gregory Brook to Blackwood

Like on so many other mornings on the Walk, we were once again woken by the many birds, which is an ever so much nicer way of being woken than by the noise made by cars, radios, alarms, people's voices…

It was no different to what it had been like for the last week or so: it was *very, very* cold. The moist, frigid air outside the sleeping bag was really not at all conducive to getting up. Eventually, however, we had no choice other than to pull on some clothes, brave the elements and start breakfast. By the time we had eaten and strapped on our packs it was almost eight o'clock.

After only an hour on the Track, we could see that it was going to be a beautiful, sunny day. With the Track moving fairly consistently in a northerly direction, we climbed up, and then down, a number of rather large hills. Two thirds of the way to our destination, we began our descent into the Blackwood Valley, where we were surrounded by beautiful jarrah and karri forests. In fact, most of this eighteen-kilometre walk was through forest areas with very tall trees, but there were also areas of waterbush, which is a type of flowering plant that belongs to the pea family, and which has small yellow and red flowers when it is in bloom. There was also a lot of soap bush. Soap bush usually grows in dense thickets; when the leaves are rubbed between the hands with water they produce a kind of soapy lather.

In the more open areas, we saw grass trees, often clumped together in small communities. Many of them had a thick stumpy black base, surmounted by a proliferation of long thin needle-like leaves that looked like hair sprouting from the head of some forest troll; others simply had the troll-like hair, while the actual base was well and truly hidden under the ground. Long flower spikes (up to three or four metres in height) stuck up here and there from among the leaves, excruciatingly thin sentries guarding the community.

We reached a gravel road, which, though it was still mainly a descent, proved to be really difficult to negotiate as the gravel was extremely loose; like the gumnuts (which had been exasperatingly difficult all day), it was the cause of several hair-raising slides. At Southampton Bridge, we took a very welcome break for about half an hour while we picked and ate blackberries, choosing to ignore all the negatives we had heard about blackberry bushes and concentrating only on the positives. The berries were prolific and quite delicious.

We then followed the Track along the riverside, through grasses and past even more blackberry bushes. We also noticed lots of emu droppings which possibly indicated that emus also like the little black berries.

Eventually the Track started to wind up a hill, aptly named Cardiac Hill. It was very, very steep, and even though there were rock steps at certain points, which gave the option for the occasional short, but much-needed, respite, the one-kilometre climb to the top really has to be experienced to be believed. When we had all finally dragged ourselves on to the summit, we were rewarded with absolutely fantastic views over the sea of pine plantations below. While we were catching our breath, we could hear the muted sounds of timber logging in the distance.

The shelter itself is perched on the edge of the hill, looking out over the plantations, and it is nestled between some very tall pines; because of the fire risk, no fires are permitted at the campsite.

We were all fairly exhausted after the climb, but the afternoon was still quite young, and the sun was pleasantly warm, so we dumped our packs in the shelter and each of us found a grassy place where we could stretch out and soak up the warmth of the sun. Much later, we made a list of all the things we needed to buy in Balingup, before attending to dinner and, finally, slipping into our sleeping bags.

It was an exceptionally beautiful spot. A haze came up from the valley just before sunset, which made the sun appear like a huge red ball hanging in the sky. It was an incredible feeling to be in such a wonderful place, with no one else anywhere, just us.

Day Twenty-Eight
Friday 15th April

Blackwood to Balingup

We managed to get up, have breakfast, pack and leave the shelter by 6.45. It was cold, and there was a lot of mist, but the forest, even with the mist, or *because* of the mist, was exceptionally beautiful. The shapes of trees disappearing into the grey haze gave everything a very eerie, other-worldly feeling. As we probably should have expected, the hills continued, even after Blackwood; on the positive side, we were treated to some magnificent views over the valley.

After leaving the campsite, the Track made a wide swing towards the east before, after about five kilometres, swinging back towards the north.

We stopped at nine-thirty for a short rest break, and, by the time we were back on the Track, the mist had well and truly evaporated. The forest had now became more open, and the seemingly endless corridors of waterbush had suddenly disappeared.

We were quite relieved that the final seven kilometres into Balingup were more or less downhill, and, though we must have missed a couple of Track signs, we managed to continue in the right direction along a sealed road. Walking on sealed roads is not particularly pleasant: the surface is usually hard, and there is always the added concern of meeting traffic. It can also be a step closer to all those things that belong to the negative side of what is known as *progress*, something that a track running through the bush or the forest is usually able to avoid.

Missing the signs meant that we bypassed the Golden Valley Tree Park, where (so we later heard) there are hundreds of specially cultivated trees and a number of picnic spots.

We arrived at Balingup Backpackers just before noon. Accommodation is in the back part of the post office; it is not very big, fitting eight guests at the most, but it is rather cute, and we were the only guests. Once upon a time, it would have been the residential part of the post office, but the present owners live elsewhere.

The post office proprietor, Andrew, was planning an afternoon trip to Bunbury (a port city 70 kilometres to the west of Balingup and 175 km south of Perth), and Jonathan decided to go with him. There was nowhere in Balingup where it was possible to download images, and Jonathan was also hoping to be able to access the Internet in Bunbury, as the computer at the post office was not working.

Before they could leave, Andrew had arranged to have his hair cut in the laundry by an itinerant hairdresser, then his wife had her hair cut. Even after the hairdresser had packed up and said goodbye, there were still several things demanding Andrew's attention, but, eventually, everything came together, and he and Jonathan left the post office just before one-thirty. I then borrowed the washing machine and did some washing, but as luck would have it the rain came down just as I was unloading the machine, and I had to hang everything on the back veranda. With the washing doing its level best to dry, Andris and I left the Backpackers, and went to have a look at the centre of Balingup.

Balingup, named after the Balingup Pool (*Balingup* is either derived from the name of a Noongar warrior, or else it comes from the Noongar word *balinga* 'to climb') is a small town on the now closed-down railway line between Perth and Albany. The main activities are farming – fruit and vegetable, beef cattle and dairy – although there is also some arts and crafts activity, a number of artists and craft people having moved into the area over recent years.

As could be expected, we discovered a few craft shops as well as a bakery, and then we visited a rather strange place where it was possible to buy pasties, coffee, cakes and some tinned stuff with labels written in Italian. It was a very dark, old-fashioned shop, and the tins, together with a few bags of dry produce like flour, rice and lentils, were all carefully displayed on long shelves. We bought some lentils and then went to the general store, which was part of the service station.

By the time we got back from our excursion, Jonathan and Andrew had returned from Bunbury, and it was not long afterwards that Andrew and his wife locked up the post office and left. As evening was beginning to fall, Andris, Jonathan and I sought out the town's only café, where we celebrated Jonathan's birthday, which was the following day. With mains and sweets, it was an amazing amount of food compared with what we normally ate; the service was good and the celebration was an enjoyable highlight, not only for Jonathan's birthday but also to mark the end of the second phase of our Walk.

After dinner, Andris returned to the post office accommodation to attend to the still wet washing (the few hours on the back veranda having been either too short or too cold to have had much effect), while Jonathan and I went to the service station to buy some orange juice as well as more methylated spirits for our stove. When we finally arrived back at the Balingup Backpackers, Andris had made up the fire in the lounge room and was in the process of drying the clothes.

It was lovely and warm in the lounge room, and we sat

around for quite some time talking. By the time the clothes had finished drying, and we were able to get our packs ready for the following morning, it was very late (for us); in fact, when we finally fell into bed, it was well after ten.

I woke around one-thirty to the sound of a clock ticking. I was confused, there being no clock in the room where we were, but, before my imagination had managed to gallop off along some dark path, I realized that it was the clock in the post office and that the place was not haunted after all.

Section Three

Balingup to Kalamunda

The third and final section of the Bibbulmun Walk, Balingup to Kalamunda, is just over four hundred kilometres in length, and it runs though the hilly areas of the Darling Ranges, where there are a number of rather high peaks to be crossed. The entire section from Balingup to Kalamunda is covered with jarrah forests and small timber, with large expanses of granite in the higher areas.

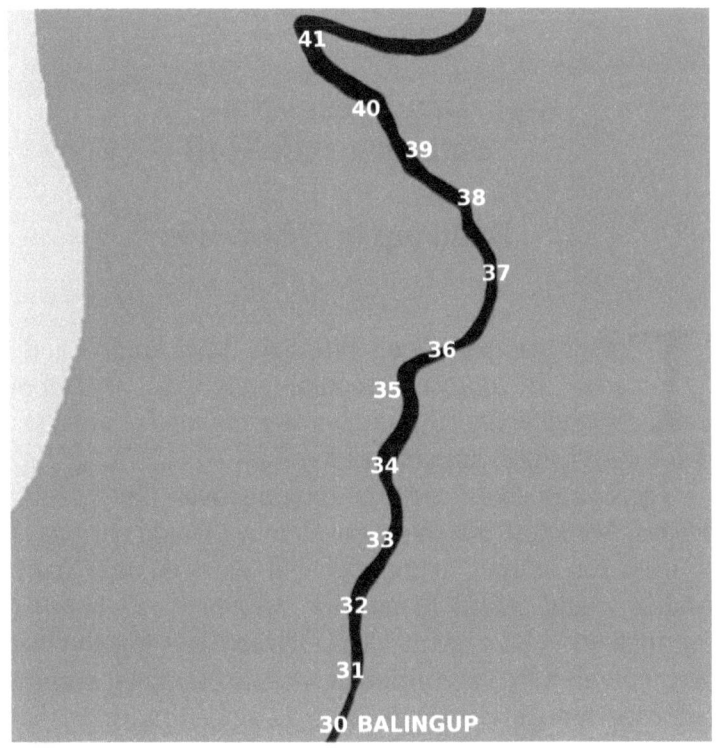

Balingup to Dwellingup 204 kilometres

30	*Balingup*	36	Yourdamung
31	Grimwade	37	Possum Springs
32	Noggerup	38	Dookanelly
33	Yabberup	39	Murray
34	*Collie*	40	Swamp Oak
35	Harris Dam	*41*	*Dwellingup*

(Italics indicate hotel or backpacker accommodation).

Day Twenty-Nine
Saturday 16th April

Balingup to Grimwade

Today was Jonathan's birthday. After Andris and I gave an almost acceptable rendition of *Happy Birthday*, we all sat down to a wonderful breakfast of toast, tomatoes, hommus and coffee.

There was some sadness hanging over the morning because we knew that this was where we would part ways, at least for a time. After eighteen days on the Track, Andris would return home, and Jonathan and I would continue on to Kalamunda. The eighteen days together had been coloured by very different kinds of weather, scenery and experiences, but all three of us agreed that they had been wonderful.

Although Jonathan and I knew that we would have to push off early, Andris would not be leaving Balingup until about one in the afternoon, when he would catch a bus to Bunbury. He was hoping that the train was again running between Bunbury and Perth, otherwise the only other alternative would be a bus. All going well, he would be in Perth around three-thirty. After a night at the same youth hostel where he stayed at the end of March, he would have a whole day to look around Perth before flying back to Sydney on the evening of the 17th.

I set out just before eight, and Andris walked with me to the end of the road where we said goodbye. I was relieved that everything had gone well with Andris and that he had had no reoccurrence of any of his health problems. Even if he would not be walking the entire Track, he had at least walked part of it and had shared so very many special experiences with us. He would now be able to relate better to those experiences that Jonathan and I had had earlier on the Track (as well as to all those experiences we had yet to experience).

It was cold and, once again, fairly misty, but the walking itself was quite pleasant. I reflected on the fact that Jonathan and I had now been walking for a month and that we still had at least two weeks of walking left to reach Kalamunda.

I was on my own: Jonathan had not yet left Balingup. I met a man and a woman out walking their dog, and they were interested to know from where I had walked and how much of the Track I was doing. When I explained that my son and I had walked from Albany and were on our way to Kalamunda, they were quite impressed. I met them again a little later on, and they had evidently been thinking about what I had told them because the man asked me if we *really* enjoyed walking so far and what it *really* felt like, walking all the time.

I can no longer remember exactly what I told them, but I assume that I said something to the effect that we were enjoying it, in spite of all the ups and downs, both physical and psychological. Dramatic changes in the weather, unexpected diversions, heavy packs and even difficult terrain are unimportant when weighed against the solitude and freedom of the actual Walk. All the difficult things that impinge on the Track and on the Walk itself are mere externals to the central, important reality which is just another variation of freedom.

I crossed the footbridge over Balingup brook and then climbed a very steep hill, where, just after nine-thirty and unbeknown to me at the time, I missed a Waugal. Still believing that I was on the Track, I actually felt quite pleased and believed that I was making good time. It started to spit rain, and I stopped and changed into wet-weather gear. It was then that it suddenly occurred to me that I was most probably on the wrong path because I had not seen any Waugals, or any other signs for that matter, for quite some time. I retraced my steps for at least one kilometre. When I finally saw a sign (which I wrongly assumed was the one I must have missed), it was actually a sign pointing back to Balingup.

I have no idea how I could have been so disorientated. Whether it was saying goodbye to Andris, or simply a case of being inattentive to the Track with my feet on the ground and my head elsewhere. Whatever the reason for my confusion, I clambered back down the hill without reflecting on the fact that I had already walked UP that very same hill about an hour earlier. It was not until I saw the bridge at the bottom of the hill that I understood what I had done, and at that point I almost burst into tears.

I had still not seen Jonathan, and I assumed that he would have to be well ahead of me (having most probably passed me after I took the first wrong turn). Struggling up the hill once more, I met three walkers coming down the hill, and they assured me that they had not seen Jonathan; in fact, they had not seen anyone. Was he in front of me or was he behind me? I had no idea. I found the Waugal that I had previously missed and got myself on to the right Track. Everything finally seemed to have sorted itself, but I had already lost at least an hour with all the wrong turns and all the backtracking.

Bridge over Balingup brook

The Track, which was relatively easy walking, wound through many different kinds of vegetation: tall forest trees, plantation pines, banksias and even soap bush; there were also lots of different birds, including many green parrots and magpies. After passing a couple of small farmhouses, I began to climb upwards, and it was then that I missed another sign, which had become completely overgrown and had disappeared into the undergrowth.

Fortunately, I quickly understood what I had done, but by that stage I had already reached the top of a hill that I should not have climbed, and yet again, I was forced to reverse my steps.

Time was now becoming extremely important: I knew that if Jonathan was in front of me, which he most probably was, he would worry if he got to the shelter ahead of me and I was not there. It began to rain before easing off and then threatening a repeat performance. Weather, however, was the very least of my worries. I knew that I dared not stop, not even to change into my wet-weather gear. I could only think of Jonathan arriving at the shelter and not finding me there. I was extremely worried, and my anxiety was increasing by the minute.

Then, just after three in the afternoon, Jonathan appeared before me on the Track. He had reached the shelter and, leaving his pack, had backtracked for about four kilometres looking for me.

All the anxiety of the last few hours came together in one enormous rush, and I burst into tears. In between sobs, I tried to explain to him what had happened and just how much I appreciated his coming back to find me. The fact that it was his birthday simply made it all the more upsetting. As always, he was extremely laid-back about it all, and, while he was assuring me that it was something that could happen to anyone, he took my pack, and we continued on to the campsite.

Later, I calculated that if I had walked somewhere between twenty-six and twenty-eight kilometres that day, Jonathan had certainly done well in excess of thirty.

Day Thirty
Sunday 17th April

Grimwade to Noggerup

The temperature on the morning of our thirtieth day on the Track was definitely no more than 7°C and for us, used to a fairly moderate climate, that was absolutely FREEZING. The birds must have been really cold as well because they did not start singing as early as they usually did of a morning. Even the kookaburras were late. On top of everything, the sunrise was quite red, and I could not help but think of the second part of the old rhyme:... *Red sky in the morning, a sailor's warning...*

As the sky began to lighten, we heard a lonely crow at least trying to make a brave, but awkward, attempt to welcome the morning.

We got away at eight. Although I desperately wanted to keep wearing my jumper, I knew that once we started walking, I would most certainly warm up, and, if I was wearing my jumper, I would have to stop and remove it. Nevertheless, strapping on a pack over a thin T-shirt on a very cold morning is definitely not one of the easiest things I have had to do. Before we had managed to thaw out to the point where we could actually feel all our fingers and toes, Jonathan began having problems with one of his boots, so we stopped briefly near a thicket of soap bush, while he did what he could to fix it.

Around eleven it looked as though it could very possibly rain, but we were hoping that if we remained optimistic and focused on only positive, sunny thoughts, it might hold off. A bit later on, with rain still threatening, we finally stopped by the side of the Track and ate some leftovers from the night before, wrapped up in bread that we had bought in Balingup. Bread does not react well to being carried in a pack; apart from drastically changing its physical appearance, it usually only lasts for about a day. Most of the time we made do with hard crispbread.

Two walkers from the north, carrying light daypacks, met us further along on the Track; they both seemed very friendly and obviously enjoyed being able to stop and talk for a while. That morning they had started out from the Mumballup Forrest Tavern, having arranged for their wives to pick them up on the road just past Grimwade later in the day. They told us that they were doing just a small part of the Walk, but they were doing it in style. One of the men had a daughter living in Balingup, where they were all staying, and, while the women did other things, the men were walking different parts of the Track each day.

Fortunately for us, the rain did not eventuate: the heavy clouds suddenly disappeared, and the sun came out. No longer having to worry about the weather, we could concentrate on the Track, which was still winding through reasonably hilly areas covered with soap bush and banksia as well as jarrah and yarri. Everywhere we could see signs of a not-so-recent bush fire, though blackened trunks were already confidently sprouting new growth, and clumps of bright green grasses were beginning to dominate the charred earth.

The Track

For a short period, we lost the Track, but at least this time we were lost together, so the anxiety factor was considerably less.

We reached the campsite just after three in the afternoon. It was a particularly nice spot, in the middle of a jarrah forest, and, as it was still sunny, we opened our packs on the grass and lay out some of our clothes and our sleeping bags on surrounding bushes to air. While we were organizing our places in the shelter, we noticed that there was a colony of bees in one corner, near the roof, but the bees, probably used to a fairly regular stream of visitors to their shelter, decided to keep to themselves, and we had more or less nothing to do with them.

During the night we were, however, kept awake by an adventurous little mouse. An obviously very hungry little mouse, she managed to eat part of a muesli bar I had in my pack as well as quite a lot of Jonathan's raisins.

Day Thirty-One
Monday 18th April

Noggerup to Yabberup to Collie

Once again, it was a very cold morning. According to our calculations, it had dropped a further whole degree to 6C°, so it did not surprise us at all that the birds and kookaburras were late again. Nevertheless, we managed to get away by eight, and as we got into a walking rhythm, we slowly began to thaw out.

The Track wound its way up and down a number of small hills and finally cut across private property. Here we walked for several kilometres along the edge of paddocks before heading down a very long hill to the Mumballup Forrest Tavern (or the Mumby Pub as it is known locally). We arrived there just after nine-thirty, which was probably a tad early in the day for a pub.

The place had the appearance of not having fully woken up; nothing much seemed to be happening, except for a man out the front unloading some things from a truck. When we stuck our heads around the door of the pub, we noticed a couple of women cleaning tables, but from what we could see, there were no customers. In short, the place had a rather depressing feel about it.

In spite of our feelings about the place, when the

telephone outside the pub proved not to be working, the man doing the unloading suggested that I use the phone inside, and I made a very brief call to Andris. He was now back in Kariong, having arrived home very early that same morning, and he managed to tell me that the trip had gone well, before my money ran out and I had to end the call.

When we bought some toasted sandwiches and a couple of bottles of orange juice, we were, without a doubt, the pub's first customers of the day. By the time we had finished eating, the morning was a good half an hour older; we shouldered our packs and set off along the Track towards Yabberup, which, according to the map, was twelve kilometres further north.

It was quite hilly with many more ascents than descents (though I am not quite sure how such a thing is even possible). After walking for about four kilometres beyond Forrest Tavern, we met four hikers coming from Yabberup. They stopped and asked us if it was far to the next campsite, but whether or not they felt that ten kilometres was far or not they did not say.

Just before noon, we stopped very briefly at Glen Mervyn Dam; we had no intention of staying very long, as we both wanted to get to the shelter as early as possible. We crossed the wall of the dam and then continued along the Track. The dam was not full, but the blue of the water that was there contrasted with the orange of the sand, forming many dramatic, colourful patterns.

Glen Mervyn Dam

The Track closely followed the dam, which is quite large, for at least two kilometres. The vegetation along the edge of the dam, and next to the Track, was a mixture of pine and low bushes, but, unfortunately, although the natural environment was extremely beautiful, the place itself was absolutely *filthy:* it would have to have been the dirtiest place we encountered on the entire Walk. I believe that the Glen Mervyn Dam is a popular caravan and camping spot, and perhaps that was the reason why the ground was littered with toilet paper, bottles, lolly wrappers, Kleenex, many discarded milk cartons, empty cigarette packets, drink cans and plastic bags. It was a dreadful pity, given the unbelievable scenic beauty of the place. The only other place that came anywhere close to the Glen Mervyn Dam from the point of view of pollution was a part of the Track between One Tree Bridge to Donnelly River Village, another area popular with tourists.

About one hundred metres from the shelter, we were met by two CALM trucks, which was definitely not something that we were expecting in the middle of the Track. One of the men hopped down from his truck and told us that they had actually been waiting there just for us. I froze just a little and wondered why just *us*, but, before my imagination had fully wrapped itself around his words, the man told us that we would be unable to remain in the area as they were about to start an extensive back-burning operation. They had known that we were on the Track and that we would be turning up at the shelter, thanks to the daily registration records kept at the campsites. They would, no doubt, have checked the logbook at the Noggerup shelter.

After talking to one of the men, Jonathan took the co-ordinates of the campsite – Andris had been collecting them while he was with us and had asked Jonathan to note down the remainder for him. When Jonathan was finished, the man then drove us (with our packs in the back of the truck) to Collie. There was no other choice available: I really do not feel that our removal from the area was in any way negotiable.

Some time after the man had left us in Collie and returned to his mates, we noticed how, once the back-burning began, the whole area behind us quickly filled with smoke. We knew then that even had it been remotely possible to have continued along the Track, it would not have been much fun.

The man from CALM seemed quite pleasant; also, from the way he talked about it, he obviously enjoyed his job. We drove over part of the Track on which we had already walked and finally turned off on to another track, which then joined up with the sealed road that led into the town. The man pointed out some of the hotels, before leaving us on the side of the road and returning to his more important task of back-burning. We decided to stay at the Crown hotel, even though our very kind firefighter did warn us that it had a reputation for being rather noisy.

Collie is a small coal-mining town. The population in 2011 was almost 7,000, so in 2005 it was probably about the same or a little less. The name *Collie* comes from the Collie River, which was named after Dr Alexander Collie, who was one of the first European explorers in the area in the late 1820s. For many years, apart from the river being given a European name, nothing else changed in the area; then, sixty years further on, coal was discovered, and the town suddenly came into being. Coal mining is still the main industry, and, with its three power stations, Collie is a leading electricity provider for the entire state.

By the time we had checked into the hotel, it was getting close to three in the afternoon. We showered and then Jonathan started the washing machine (which we were allowed to use), and as there was no dryer we hung everything on lines behind the hotel. Later, Jonathan accessed the Internet at the local library, and I found a place where I was able to download images to a disc, before posting the disc home. I had just started shopping for supplies when Jonathan joined me around five-thirty, half an hour before the shop was due to close. We took advantage of the public phone and phoned the motel in Dwellingup to say that we were not sure whether we would arrive there on the Saturday or the Sunday, and they assured us that either would be okay; then we returned to the hotel and sorted the shopping into our packs. The clothes were, not surprisingly, still wet, so Jonathan strung up a couple of lines across the room, and we turned on both the heater and the fan with the window closed.

Towards evening, we went down to the dining room to eat, but the place was quite unattractive, and no one seemed the least bit interested in taking our order, so I suggested to Jonathan that we try elsewhere. We went to the Chinese restaurant next door and received not only wonderful service but also enormous meals.

By the time we had eaten and sorted a few things, it was well after nine, and I went to bed. Jonathan, on the other hand, took himself to the little breakfast room at the end of the corridor, where he spent some time working out all the map co-ordinates.

After sleeping outdoors in the cold for so long, it was understandably very hot in the room, especially with the window closed and the heater going.

Day Thirty-Two
Tuesday 19th April

Collie to Harris Dam

We were already wide awake before six, and after having dressed and crammed our now dry clothing into our packs we had our continental breakfast in the breakfast room. According to a sign on the wall, the hotel had won a prize in 2000 for the best renovated hotel. As I looked at the sign, I could not help but wonder what the worst renovated hotel had looked like. Apart from the unattractive dining area, the women's bathroom area, at least on our floor, was temporarily unisex. After we had checked into the hotel, I discovered that what would normally have been the women's bathroom was also open to men simply because I was the only woman on that floor. This was a worry in itself, but it was exacerbated by the fact that there was no lock on the shower door or, for that matter, on the bathroom door itself. The concerns about privacy to one side, the bathroom itself was definitely not somewhere where one would be happy to linger: it had that cold, impassive stone appearance that many public bathrooms seem to have, and one of the bathroom taps leaked incessantly. In fact, everything about the hotel was very depressing and grey.

We left the hotel at eight and, having slept in an overly warm room, were slightly shocked by how awfully COLD it was outside, the sky being completely clear and cloud-free.

For the first eight kilometres or so, I felt that the Track was simply twisting and turning in on itself, which, as far as I was concerned, meant that we were walking twice as far as we would have been doing had we been walking in a straight line; however, when I checked the map, I discovered that this was not the case at all, so perhaps it had more to do with the fact that we were still adjusting to the cold and less to do with reality.

After walking due west beyond the town, we very soon turned towards the north, and the Track continued in a fairly consistent northerly direction until just before Harris Dam when it took a definite swing towards the east. The guide book advised us to pay close attention to Track signs and to keep the guide book and map handy, especially during the first part of the walk beyond Collie, as a multitude of small vehicle tracks could possibly cause some confusion. As always, we kept the guide book handy, but for some strange reason this was one part of the Walk where we did not have any problem keeping to the correct Track.

During the morning, we took a couple of breaks; I was again having problems with my feet, and I changed from my boots into my sandals. Later, we met a fellow coming from Harris Dam on his way towards Collie, and he told us that he had already met a couple a few kilometres ahead of us and that they were also on their way to Harris Dam.

We finally caught up with them around two in the afternoon near the Worsley Alumina conveyor (a 52-kilometre conveyor that carries bauxite from the mine near Boddington to the refinery at Worsley). From what I have heard, it is one of the longest conveyor belts in the world.

The couple, Brian and Janette from England, were also doing the whole Track from Albany to Kalamunda. It was very refreshing to be able to talk to people doing the whole Track in the same direction as we were doing it because they were few and far between. Although Brian and Janette soon moved off in the direction of Harris Dam, we decided to take a short break, knowing that we would soon catch up with our new friends at the campsite.

We arrived at Harris Dam at exactly 14.46 to find Brian sitting among the trees in front of the shelter, enjoying a portable foot bath: a bit of on-track luxury that probably made a lot of sense.

Harris Dam is a really beautiful campsite, and the shelter itself is the type where the sleeping platform is divided into two, with a space in between for the table and benches. On each side of the shelter, there is a bunk-type arrangement, where there is an extra-wide platform above the normal sleeping platform, accessible by a ladder. This means that, in such a shelter, there are four separate sleeping platforms, two up and two down, and the shelter would probably house eight people quite comfortably. As it turned out, being only four people, we each had our own sleeping space.

The last few shelters had all been of a similar design, whereas the earlier shelters used a single large platform. Usually, the roof of such shelters juts out at the front to give some protection to the table and benches at the front of the shelter.

Harris Dam campsite

We sat and talked with Brian and Janette for quite some time after dinner. It was a beautiful evening, and the fact that we were completely surrounded by forest simply added to the enjoyment. In the distance, we could hear the constant, dull hum of the conveyor, the only reminder that there was something called *civilization* somewhere beyond the edges of the campsite and the forest.

The next day we were planning a double-walking day: 32.2 kilometres.

Day Thirty-Three
Wednesday 20th April

Harris Dam to Yourdamung to Possum Springs

We left Harris Dam before seven, taking farewell of our two new friends, who had no intention of doubling up. We were confident that we would manage the thirty-plus kilometres in good time, even though early on – yes, you guessed it – we missed a sign and had to retrace about 500 metres.

After leaving the camp, the Track followed an easterly direction for almost three kilometres before swinging around to the north-east.

The walking was both pleasant and easy, and we reached Yourdamung just after ten o'clock, by which time it was definitely starting to warm up. We ate some leftovers from the previous evening, and then continued on to Possum Springs around eleven. I was, however, still having a problem with my feet, and I spent much of the day alternating between my boots and sandals.

By the time we got back on the Track, it was really quite hot (about 29°C), and it was not long before the vegetation had changed to swamp vegetation with some paperbacks, grass trees and swamp banksia, none of which afforded much shade. Not having thought to fill up my water bottles at Yourdamung, I was trying my best to preserve the very little water I had left.

The swamp vegetation gradually merged with areas of old-forest trees, which, thankfully, gave us some shade. After we had managed more than half the distance to Possum Springs, with only seven kilometres of fairly hilly walking left, we took a second short break.

Grass trees

We finally reached the shelter just before four, by which time there were already two other people at the campsite. They introduced themselves as Brett and Di, and, as they were using a tent, the shelter was all ours.

After thirty-two kilometres, we were quite tired, and not long after eating dinner we were already zipped into our sleeping bags. Before falling asleep, I vaguely noticed that it was almost full moon and, for a change, not overly cold.

Day Thirty-Four
Thursday 21st April

Possum Springs to Dookanelly

There was to be no doubling up today, so we were focusing on a walk of less than twenty kilometres. Also, it was not as hot; in fact, it even looked as though it could rain. I was becoming quite convinced that there were only three weather patterns to choose between: very hot, freezing cold or teeming rain.

We left Possum Springs at seven, and the walking was great, in spite of the fact that there were many rather challenging hills, especially the closer we came to Dookanelly. After about seven kilometres we passed under the Worsley Alumina conveyor for the second time, but this time, for some unknown reason, it was not in operation. A kilometre or so further on, we took a short break near the Murray River. We then crossed the historic Long Gully Bridge, which is a 128-metre-long wooden trestle bridge built in 1949 by the Western Australian Government Railways. It was initially used to transport timber, but, since 1998, it has been used exclusively by walkers.

In February 2015, bush fires raged across almost 100,000

hectares of Western Australia's south-west, destroying many properties as well as wiping out huge areas of forest and farmland, and the Long Gully Bridge was destroyed. Apart from the tragedy of losing a structure of such historical significance, the bridge was the only way for walkers to cross the Murray River, and was an essential part of the Bibbulmun Walk. Without the bridge it is not possible, at the moment of writing (2015), to walk end-to-end, though it is more likely that some kind of diversion will eventually be put in place[5].

Along the Track, we saw many red-tailed black cockatoos as well as a lot of very live kangaroos and, unfortunately, one dead kangaroo. When Brett and Di later caught up with us at the campsite, they excitedly told us that they had also seen emus.

Arriving at the shelter at 12.30, we unstrapped our packs, and then I swept the shelter (every shelter has a broom just for this purpose). Having selected our corners of the shelter and rolled out our sleeping mats and sleeping bags, we filled in the log book, sorted out what we were making for that evening's dinner and began writing out a shopping list for when we were to reach Dwellingup in a day's time; we were already considering doubling up the following day.

---

[5] In 2017 a new state-of-the-art suspension bridge opened 12 kilometres downstream from the old bridge. Check the Bibbulmun website for track changes.

Long Gully Bridge 2005

Although it seems quite unbelievable, the shelter at Dookanelly, more or less in the middle of nowhere, actually has electricity. We were fascinated when we saw the power point but soon noticed that that was all there was: there were no lights connected to the outlet. Apart from the wall socket, which probably worked with electrical appliances (of which we had none), there was also a mirror, a wall clock and a bookcase, so the Dookanelly campsite was definitely very upmarket. A sign said that it had been built by the aluminium company, which probably accounted for all the little extras.

The problem with my feet had not gone away, so I changed some of the Fixomull bandages and then removed the nails from both of my big toes. Although it probably sounds quite disgusting, the nails had both died and were pushing against the toes themselves, which, in turn, was impacting on walking. After this fairly primitive medical procedure, I was already looking forward to problem-free walking the following day.

Brett and Di arrived an hour or so after us, and because it was looking like rain they also decided to sleep in the shelter. We made dinner, after which we sat around and talked for a bit before rolling ourselves up in our sleeping bags. When the kookaburras began their strange call fifteen minutes before the onset of darkness, Brett told us that kookaburras were actually not endemic to Western Australia but were introduced from the eastern states. He also told us that the red-tailed black cockatoo is endangered, and that the area through which we were all walking is supposed to be the wettest, coldest part of Western Australia.

Day Thirty-Five
Friday 22nd April

Dookanelly to Murray to Swamp Oak

With another double day ahead of us we left just after seven, not before taking farewell of our overnight friends. As they were not doubling up, it was most unlikely that we would be meeting up with them again.

We started off with a short ascent away from the campsite, and after a few kilometres on vehicle tracks we eventually had a very long descent to the Murray River Fireline. The fireline is a cleared wide track that more or less parallels most of the Track to the Murray campsite, before looping off to the west and then swinging back to the Track near Swamp Oak.

The guide book had told us that the Murray River Fireline is often used by fishermen and non-walkers, especially during the summer; however, given the fact that we were already a couple of months into autumn, we did not expect to meet up with anyone, fishermen or otherwise.

After about three or four kilometres, we reached the Murray River, which the Track then followed in a north-easterly direction, all the way to the Murray campsite.

The heavy undergrowth made it very difficult to see much of the river, even though we knew that it was there; the terrain, on the other hand, was reasonably flat, and we reached Murray just after eleven-thirty. We had heard that this particular area is renowned for very high rainfall, but we had managed to reach the first campsite of the day without so much as a drop, and we were hoping that our luck might continue for the rest of the day.

We stopped at the Murray campsite shelter, ate some lunch and then rested for about thirty minutes. Some time after twelve, knowing that we still had at least nineteen kilometres to manage before dark, we set off for Swamp Oak. Fortunately, the weather was not too hot, with the temperature in the low twenties.

The easy walking continued beyond the Murray River camp, and even though we were doubling up it did not feel at all difficult. Also, the fact that my feet were feeling really good again added to the enjoyment, and our luck as regards the weather continued to hold. We passed through many different landscapes: small hills, rail formations and a number of areas that had previously been laid waste by bush fires. She-oaks, banksias and karri were the main vegetation, alongside of several large forests.

As it turned out, everything was just too good to last, and not long before we reached Swamp Oak we came face to face with some dreadfully steep hills. On the worst one of them there was actually a sign telling us how much further it was to the shelter – *7 km to Swamp Oak*. Signs giving the distance to campsites are not common practice on this Walk, and we decided that someone must have decided that a small degree of moral support was needed just at that particular point.

At four o'clock, we were still three kilometres from the campsite, and we arrived at the shelter at five-thirty, just as darkness was about to fall. That it had taken one and a half hours to walk those three kilometres is probably indicative of the terrain and our state of fatigue.

As we regained our composure, we noticed that we were not the only people at the campsite: two men and a dog had obviously arrived before us and were already finishing their meal. We spoke to them briefly and then set about making dinner. It turned out that the two men were only on an overnight camping excursion, and, as they had food left over, they kindly gave us two tomatoes and some broccoli – I never knew that tomatoes could taste or smell so wonderful. It is not possible to carry fruit or vegetables (other than the dehydrated kind), as things like tomatoes or bananas would no longer look like tomatoes or bananas after a couple of days of being squeezed into a pack.

We were still drinking our tea and coffee as darkness definitely closed in on us. Once again it was a beautiful evening, and the moon, which was almost full, was very red. Finally, the rain that had very considerately held off all day began to fall, and it continued for most of the night.

Day Thirty-Six
Saturday 23rd April

Swamp Oak to Dwellingup

It was pouring when we woke up, and I feared that we were in for a solid day of rain; however, by seven, when breakfast was finished and we were about to leave the shelter, it had completely stopped.

We had only thirteen kilometres in front of us, and we were looking forward to a long, hot shower and a decent meal when we reached Dwellingup. With so much to look forward to, the initial seven or eight kilometres, which stretched across some rather challenging hills, were not quite as daunting as they could have been.

Not far beyond the campsite at Swamp Oak, we crossed a swampy area on a boardwalk, and soon afterwards the hills began. As we reached the first of the hills, we entered a devastated pine plantation bordered by dried-out, grey blackberry bushes, the result of persistent spraying. The entire area had been completely logged, and the devastation, together with all the dead, twisted bushes, painted a rather depressing picture. The plantation, or what was left it, hugged the sides of the hills, and we were very relieved when the Track finally left the plantation and moved back into the forest.

Focused as we were on both the desolation and the hills, we may have let our positive thinking dwindle a little. Just after we moved back into the forest, the rain came down again, this time with a vengeance, and it continued without any let-up all the way to Dwellingup.

Not far from the outskirts of that small village, we met a large group of bushwalkers on their way to Swamp Oak, and one of them on the tail end asked us if it was far to go. He must have known that it was at least thirteen kilometres, but, perhaps, given the weather, he was hoping for some kind of miraculous shrinkage of the distance ahead of him.

Dwellingup, from the Aboriginal word meaning 'place of nearby water' (which, in the circumstances, was rather appropriate), is a very small town with around three hundred inhabitants. The main employers are the timber and fruit-growing industries, while the very large bauxite mine at nearby Huntly (a supplier of bauxite to two aluminium refineries) also provides work for many of the locals.

We had already booked rooms at the hotel, and we were relieved to find that it was both pleasantly presented and very clean. The shower area, which is always part of the main focus after several days on the Track (the other part is the food), was all we could wish for, and a great deal more. After changing out of my very wet clothes and showering, I spent at least half an hour getting my notes up to date. It was still raining, and we were very fortunate that there was both a washing machine *and* a dryer at the hotel. After putting on a load of washing, we went over to the CALM office to find out what was happening with the

Track further ahead.

Several people had mentioned that part of the Track further north had been closed due to a bush fire that had gone through the area the previous December. The information was vague, and no one knew where the Track was closed or even if the rumours were correct. At several points along the Track, we had tried, unsuccessfully, to get an update on the situation, and we were now hoping that someone at the CALM office might be able to let us know what was actually happening.

CALM, however, was closed. As we stood outside the building, wondering why it was closed, it suddenly struck us that it was Saturday. Then we saw that the information centre was open, and our very dashed hopes began to rise a little. Unfortunately, the person on duty at the centre, although pleasant, was really not a lot of help, and we decided that the only thing we could do was to assume that everything was as it should be and that the Track was open all the way.

By now the rain was absolutely teeming down, and we were both pleased that we were not out on the Track. I posted some postcards in an old-fashioned red postbox, while Jonathan checked on the washing and the drying back at the hotel; we then met up (as previously arranged) at a small café a short walk from the hotel, where we treated ourselves to Devonshire tea. While the café inside was warm and snug, the persistent rain beat against the window panes, painting everything beyond the windows a cold watery grey. We spoke briefly with our friends from Swamp Oak, who were also at the café, having arrived in Dwellingup with their dog not long before we did.

Jonathan returned to the hotel once again to check on

the progress of the washing, and I found a public phone from where I phoned the roadhouse at North Banister. I needed to find out what kind of supplies they might have, but the answer, unfortunately, was: "None."

I then met up with Jonathan at the general store, and we did some shopping for supplies, keeping in mind that we would not be able to get anything at North Bannister. Sadly, even though Dwellingup was a step up from *none*, supplies were definitely limited, and we were trying not to spend too much time regretting that we had not stocked up with more provisions in Collie. In the circumstances, we had to very hurriedly re-invent our menus for the next few days.

When we returned to the hotel, our washing, thanks to Jonathan's supervision, was dry, and we were able to finish packing. Then, around six-thirty, we went into the dining room to have dinner. It was a pleasant room and particularly well patronized. We both ordered vegetarian lasagne with chips and vegetables and wine and finished off the meal with sticky date pudding. The food was most enjoyable and a welcome change to what we normally ate when we were on the Track.

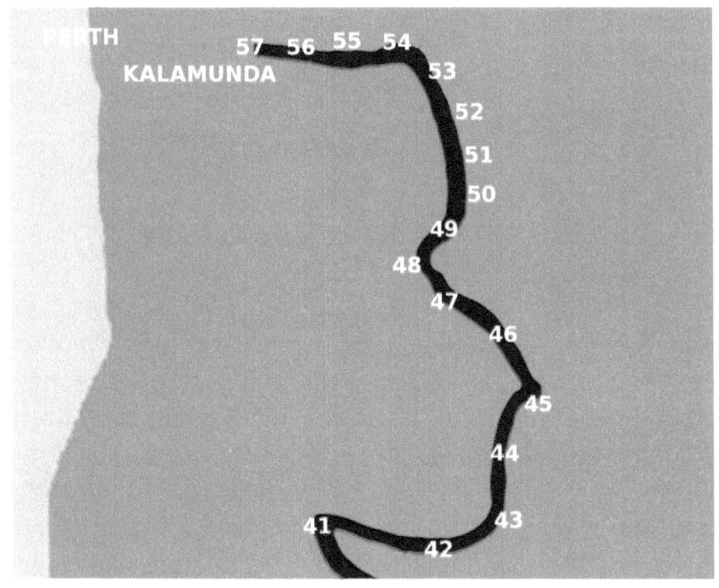

Dwellingup to Kalamunda 202 kilometres

41	*Dwellingup*	50	Brookton
42	Chadora	51	Mount Dale
43	Mount Wells	52	Beraking
44	White Horse Hills	53	Waalegh
45	Gringer Creek	54	Helena
46	Nerang	55	Ball Creek
47	Mount Cooke	56	Hewitt's Hill
48	Monadnocks	57	Kalamunda
49	Canning		

(Italics indicate hotel or backpacker accommodation).

Day Thirty-Seven
Sunday 24th April

Dwellingup to Chadoora to Mount Wells

By the time we woke up the next morning, we were greatly relieved to see that it had stopped raining, especially now when we once again had clean, dry clothes. We managed to leave the hotel just after seven-thirty, but it took us quite some time to find the way out of Dwellingup and back on to the Track. Given the size of the town, this was really quite ludicrous. After several wrong turns, we finally found all the right signs and discovered that the Track was actually following the old disused railway line, moving in a south-easterly direction.

After about three kilometres, we passed a memorial sign to Holyoake Townsite, inspiring those passing by to reflect on the small community that had existed at the site between 1910 and 1961. Holyoake was only one of a number of towns or villages, all connected with the timber industry, that sprang up around Dwellingup after the railway opened in 1910. In 1961, after half a century of successful timber milling, the entire area was razed by a dreadful bush fire. Started by lightning strikes, the fire destroyed thousands of hectares of forest, and all the small mill towns were burnt to the ground. Even Dwellingup lost many buildings.

After six more kilometres, still following the railway line, we passed the Etmilyn siding in the middle of a forest. When the steam engines were running, Etmilyn was one of a number of watering spots, the water coming from a small dam nearby. Now there is not much to see at Etmilyn, beyond the siding, but the memories are still there.

Standing in the very quiet forest, it was easy to imagine the sound of a train pulling into the siding and the voices of the men as they swung the water pipe across to the boiler, while whiffs of tobacco smoke mixed seductively with the sharp smell of coal smoke. But then, as suddenly as they came, the smells and the sounds were gone, and there was only the forest and the siding and the silence.

Eventually, eleven kilometres beyond Dwellingup, the Track parted company with the railway line and turned east towards Chadoora. During this part of the Walk we saw a wallaby; we also met a number of walkers, all of whom were coming from the direction of Chadoora.

We arrived at Chadoora just before one in the afternoon, and the campsite was already packed with several small groups and many very excited boy scouts. We had completely forgotten that the following day was Anzac Day (a day of remembrance, commemorating all Australians and New Zealanders who have served in war) and that many people would be taking advantage of the resulting long weekend. Without even discussing our revised plans with each other, we both immediately knew that we would be doubling up, even though that had definitely not been our intention from the beginning. We had some lunch and talked to a few of the people who were at the campsite and then left for Mount Wells just before one-thirty.

Fortunately, the terrain was quite flat, at least in the beginning, and the easy-walking conditions went a little way towards alleviating the fact that we now had to face an extra fifteen kilometres on top of the twenty we had already completed.

For most of those fifteen kilometres, we were walking through the same kind of vegetation – banksia, grass tree, karri – that had surrounded us for the last few days, but as we crossed a creek a few kilometres before reaching the foot of Mount Wells (and the very steep climb to the top) we came across a lot of wandoo, which is a medium-sized, smooth-bark eucalyptus. The word *wandoo* comes from the Noongar word for tree.

On our way from Chadoora to Mount Wells, we met about nine people in total, and they were all heading for the campsite at Chadoora. From what they told us, it sounded as though all of them were intending to spend the night at Chadoora, so we had absolutely no doubt as to whether or not we had made the right decision about doubling up.

During the next two and a half hours of fairly solid walking, we saw one lone emu and a lot of wallabies. Finally, we reached the base of Mount Wells, the summit looming 550 metres above us. Jonathan went on ahead, and I reached the hut (an actual hut, not just a shelter) an hour later, after a very steep, three-and-a-half-kilometre climb.

Mount Wells, the highest point in the surrounding timber-milling area, is complete with a watch tower that was built to warn of fire danger. The tower is the second highest fire tower in Western Australia, and the fire watchman used to have his own hut next to the tower; quite ironically, this hut was completely burnt down in the bush fire of 1961. It was rebuilt the following year, but as technology improved it became unnecessary to have a watchman on permanent duty, and the hut was converted into accommodation for walkers doing the Bibbulmun Track.

Another walker, Paul (walking north to south) had arrived at the hut just before us. He was in his fifties and seemed quite pleasant. When I, at long last, pulled myself

up the side of the mountain and staggered over to the hut,

Paul and Jonathan were standing outside, talking. It was, however, getting quite cold, so, after introductions and basic pleasantries, the three of us sorted out places to sleep. Although 'converted into accommodation' sounds rather promising, the inside of the hut is not much more than a shelter with four walls, which is probably a pretty good representation of the word *hut*.

By the time the sun went down it was really *very, very* cold, and I pulled on several layers of clothes before crawling into my sleeping bag; in fact, I put on practically everything I had in my pack. The full moon, the second full moon so far on our Walk, had now appeared, and Jonathan was keen to take some photos. I declined an invitation to leave the relative warmth of my sleeping bag, and he braved the top of the mountain on his own, climbing part of the way up the fire tower and taking some fantastic photos.

During the night the wind absolutely howled around the hut, and, whether it was because of the wind or not, I had some very strange dreams that kept waking me up, and Jonathan said later that he did not sleep very well either.

Day Thirty-Eight
Monday 25th April

Mount Wells to White Horse Hills

We did not get away from the hut until after seven-thirty; it was SO bitterly cold. Before we could even begin to consider any kind of walking, we had to first thaw out so that we could stand up in a vaguely perpendicular fashion and, even more importantly, use our fingers.

Paul left quite early, but even when we pushed off half an hour later it was still freezing, and we were still wearing our jumpers. This was the first time on the Walk that we actually started walking while still wearing jumpers. When it was cold of a morning, we usually kept them on while we were having breakfast and getting our packs organized, but then we took them off just before we left. Not this morning.

It took us at least half an hour to find the Track going north, so we were not particularly impressed with the signs at Mount Wells. Although the guide book, which is very good and extremely informative, does include track notes for the north-going walker, the descriptions of the Track for each separate segment are definitely designed for the walker going from north to south. We both became quite proficient at reading the book from the back to the front, but reading the description of each separate day's walk and mentally turning it upside down to equate with a south-north experience of the Track could, at times, be a little confusing. The wealth of information for the north-south walker was often disproportionate when viewed with south-north eyes: for example, there was a lot about the difficult ascent for the south-going walker coming from White Horse Hills, but nothing at all about the equally difficult ascent for the north-going walker coming from Chadoora.

Nevertheless, we eventually found the Track and started down the other side of the mountain; by this time, we were able to stop and finally remove our jumpers.

My pack was not sitting as it should, and as a result it felt twice as heavy as usual. I stopped and moved some things around, but it was still feeling uncomfortable, and after about another kilometre I was forced to stop again. This time I more or less emptied the pack and then repacked it. This seemed to work, and for the rest of the day I had no more pack problems.

After eleven kilometres (with about four more to go), we reached the White Horse Hills and started to climb. It was very open and fairly rocky, with lots of small blue flowers among the scattered brown and orange rocks. When we finally reached the top, we had amazing views in most directions, while on the summit itself there were two eagles bathing in a rock pool. It was an absolutely breathtaking image. There were also hundreds of large dragon lizards whizzing over the rocks: it felt as though we had slipped through some invisible wall in time and space, and entered another world.

By this stage, the day was absolutely beautiful: clear blue skies and a temperature in the mid-twenties. We scrambled down the other side, passing many boulders, both large and small, and arrived at the shelter just before one in the afternoon. It was a particularly nice campsite, and we had it all to ourselves. We ate some lunch, and later in the afternoon we were treated to the sight of two emus standing right next to the shelter.

White Horse Hills

Day Thirty-Nine
Tuesday 26th April

White Horse Hills to Gringer Creek

For whatever reason, the alarm clock did not ring, or perhaps it did, and we simply did not hear it (or did not want to hear it). As a result, we did not wake up until six-thirty. It was bitterly cold and very crisp; by the time we had defrosted ourselves sufficiently to make breakfast and pack up, it was already seven-thirty.

At the beginning of the day's walk, there was a fairly steep ascent, followed by a long descent; most of the time it was very misty with a soft, dewy wetness falling from the trees. We had been warned that this was one of the more difficult sections of the Track, yet we of all people managed it without any problem.

By the time we had reached the top of the first mountain, visibility, on account of the mist, was almost zero, and there was really no opportunity to take photos. We then crossed a relatively flat section before making another ascent (still very misty) and then, finally, a descent. We did not see anyone all day, but an hour or so before reaching Gringer Creek we met two women who were walking in the opposite direction.

The track finally crossed the Albany Highway, and

although there was not a lot of traffic, even the few cars that we saw seemed quite threatening. Coming from the tranquillity of the bush, I know that I felt quite unsure of myself. It had been so long since we had had to interact with anything like a highway and fast-moving traffic, and we were more than relieved to reach the other side where we could once again disappear back into the bush.

We arrived at the shelter just before noon, by which time the mist had well and truly evaporated, and the afternoon, as a result, was beautifully warm and sunny. We claimed our corners of the shelter and, leaving our packs behind, walked the short distance through the bush to the North Bannister Roadhouse. The short walk, which was over flat, sandy ground with low vegetation, took us about fifteen minutes, and we shared the space with many screeching cockatoos.

The roadhouse, an eat-in and take-away stopping point on the Albany Highway, was not going to provide us with any supplies, but we did manage to find crispbread, jelly beans, chips and methylated spirits. We were also able to buy some toasted sandwiches and lemonade for lunch, which we ate at the roadhouse. I phoned Andris, and then we returned to the shelter.

Not long after we got back to the shelter, a father and son (Paul and Hayden) arrived from the north, but we saw little of them, as they pitched their tent well behind the shelter and kept very much to themselves. While I made dinner, Jonathan returned to North Bannister to get rid of all the rubbish that we had collected since leaving Dwellingup.

Once the sun disappears, and it becomes dark, there is really not much else that one can do without any form of lighting. Reading is completely out of the question and simply sitting on a timber floor, looking out into the almost impenetrable darkness, is probably not for everyone. The most sensible thing to do is to crawl into the sleeping bag, an option, which, after a long day of walking, is usually the most attractive.

The sound of the highway dominated the night: Gringer Creek would have to be the noisiest campsite on the entire Track. The noise meant that we slept badly, which actually had a compensation of sorts; in the wee hours of the morning, we were visited by a very curious bandicoot, and had we been asleep we probably would not have seen him (or her).

Inside one of the northern huts

Day Forty
Wednesday 27th April

Gringer Creek to Nerang to Mount Cooke

During the past few weeks, we had learnt to accept that it would be freezing when we crawled out of our sleeping bags in the mornings. It was a fact of life, even if we would have liked it to be otherwise, and this morning was definitely no different. Focusing on the advantages of an early start, we tried to ignore the crisp, cold (read *ice-tinged*) air pressing in on us, and we managed to be up by six and on the Track an hour later.

It was easy, flat walking with the Track moving in a fairly consistent north-west direction. We traipsed through a lot of what looked like swamp, or would probably have been swamp had there been sufficient rain, as well as through many areas that had obviously been ravaged by bush fires. There was an abundance of cockatoos, both white and black, as well as many wallabies; also the day turned out to be delightfully sunny.

We reached Nerang just before eleven. The shelter itself was quite nice, but there were two bags of rubbish hanging on one of the walls, and we both wondered who was supposed to collect them. Perhaps, in the same way that some people walking parts of the Track actually believe that food can be purchased at the shelters, the people who left the rubbish may have truly believed that there was some kind of Bibbulmun Track Rubbish Collection Service. I could not help wondering how the collection was to be made; whether there was a devoted band of rubbish collectors marching in by foot, or whether the Collection Service possibly had access to a helicopter. I really do not know. It can be interesting and, at times, depressing to be faced with the results of how some people think.

When we were filling in the register, we noticed that someone had recently written that they had seen some emus with chicks at the campsite. It would have been lovely to have seen them, and we did keep our eyes open, but either they had all moved on or they were resting somewhere where they could not be seen.

After a short rest, we ate some lunch and were back on the Track before twelve-thirty. By this time, the sun had clouded over, and it had turned rather cool; there was even a vague hint of rain in the air, though it had not actually started to rain, and we were fervently hoping that we would manage the next thirteen kilometres without getting drenched.

The first seven or eight kilometres beyond the Nerang campsite were very flat, and the Track itself was much the same as it had been all day, but we knew that once we reached the base of Mount Cooke the terrain would change dramatically.

We were now in the Monadnocks Conservation Park, which is part of what is known as the Darling Scarp (or the Darling Ranges), and ahead of us we had the three tallest peaks in the park: Mount Cooke, Mount Vincent and Mount Cuthbert. Over the years since it was officially discovered (late 1820s) the escarpment has been exploited for its timber, its bauxite and its rock quarries. Mount Cooke, the tallest of the three peaks, is 582 metres high and is named after William Ernest Cooke, who was the first Government Astronomer.

It was a reasonably steep ascent to the summit of Mount Cooke, and as we moved upwards we could see how the surrounding countryside was slowly recovering from the disastrous bush fire that had swept through the area a couple of years earlier. Even though much of the area had regenerated, it was still possible to see many blackened trees and large swathes of bare ground where nothing much was growing.

The top of the mountain was solid rock, which would not have been the best surface for walking on a rainy day. The guide book told us that the rock is granite and that it is millions of years old, which not only takes the prize for the oldest area of granite anywhere in the world but also manages to put many other things (like freezing-cold mornings, sore feet or even raisin-eating mice) into a slightly different perspective. Sunny or rainy, standing on such a surface had to be a long way ahead of many other spiritual experiences, and coupled with the amazing feeling of being on top of the world (well, almost; everything, after all, is relative) it was a very special moment. Although there is no complete panoramic view from the actual summit, there are amazing views from several points on the way up to the top.

As we were leaving the summit, I suddenly lost sight of Jonathan. Although he had started on the descent before I did, I could not see him or his green backpack anywhere below me, and given the reasonably sparse vegetation near the summit (which meant that I *should* have been able to see him) the thought occurred to me that he may have fallen off the edge of the mountain. On second thoughts, I decided that if anyone was likely to fall off a mountain that person would have to be me. As it turned out, he had simply taken a different path down to the shelter.

After traversing the top of the saddle before descending by our separate paths, we both arrived at the shelter more or less at the same time. It was just going on four o'clock, and we were very pleased that the threat of rain had been no more than just a threat.

The 2003 fire had destroyed the shelter, which had then been rebuilt the following year, but signs of the devastation, including the burnt-out water tank, were still visible, a reminder of just how small and vulnerable we are when faced with the staggering forces of nature.

When I went to bed that night, I placed one of my water bottles next to my sleeping bag, which was a fairly normal routine; however, this time I removed the tubing without tightening the cap correctly. When I inadvertently knocked the bottle during the night, I found myself in the middle of a small lake of spreading water and had to get up and wipe up the water (as well as find a dry spot for the sleeping bag). It was clearly annoying, but fortunately the moon was still full, so at least I was able to see what I was doing.

Many years ago, when we first started long-distance hiking, Andris designed a special drinking system with tubing and a valve, so that we could have our water bottle in our pack and yet still drink from it while we were walking. We use two-litre water bottles, which, unlike most of the standard commercial water bladders, retain their shape and place in the pack even as the level of the water sinks. The system, which is simple and cheap, has been so successful that, over the years, Andris has built many such systems for other hikers who want to be able to have easy, unhindered access to water while walking.

Day Forty-One
Thursday 28th April

Mount Cooke to Monadnocks to Canning

We knew that we had another double-up day ahead of us, but by this stage of the Walk the idea of it did not cause any great concern. We had both really liked Mount Cooke; it is a lovely spot, and it would have been nice if we could have stayed longer, but, with more than twenty-eight kilometres to walk, we left the campsite by seven-thirty.

The Track moved off in a north-westerly direction through the Monadnocks Conservation Park, and for the first couple of hours we enjoyed fairly flat walking. After about seven kilometres, we began to climb Mount Vincent (486 metres), and the closer we came to the top we found that, as with Mount Cooke, we were walking on exposed granite. Once we reached the top, we moved across a saddle between Mount Vincent and Mount Cuthbert (495 metres), and it was here we met the one and only person we were to meet all morning, Mick, who was walking on his own, north to south.

The views from both Mount Cuthbert and Mount Vincent are fantastic, but we could not stay there for ever, and we reluctantly descended Mount Cuthbert, arriving at Monadnocks around eleven-thirty. Sometime during the hour we spent at the campsite, a party of walkers doing a four-day circle walk from Sullivan Rock arrived.

We had walked not much more than a kilometre beyond Monadnocks, when I managed to trip over a root that very inconveniently stuck up in the middle of the path. The fall with a full pack was quite unpleasant, but the damage was minimal. Shaken, with a ripped trouser leg and a bleeding knee, but otherwise none the worse for wear, I re-collected myself, shouldered the pack, and we pushed on through the national park; we still had fifteen kilometres left to the next campsite, Canning.

We encountered a number of watercourses of varying sizes, and after about eight kilometres we reached the Canning River, where we saw lots of cockatoos and wallabies.

The Track crossed the river on a footbridge that had been built high above the water, no doubt to allow for possible flooding during the rainy season. Once we had reached the other side, we very soon entered an extensive area of she-oaks and jarrah.

Closer to the campsite, a detour had recently been put in place after someone had burnt down a bridge over a small stream. Whether the fire had been intentional or accidental was a question to which we had no answer. However, the more we thought about it, we decided that it would have had to be intentional, as it would be fairly difficult to accidentally burn down a bridge. The resulting detour was fairly uninteresting walking, but it actually saved us around two kilometres, and we reached the shelter just after four in the afternoon.

After making dinner on our little stove, I borrowed Jonathan's sewing equipment (for whatever reason this was one of the things I had failed to pack, probably because I had not expected to be doing any sewing) and mended my trousers.

The forest surrounding the shelter was not particularly dense, and yet, for some reason, the whole area felt extremely weird, almost eerie. Whether this somewhat frightening feeling was caused by the combination of grass trees, banksias and blackened trees around the campsite, or whether it was because of all of that plus something else, I am not sure. There was also a definite sensation of imminent rain. Although this sensation was proven wrong, and it did not rain, we were later visited by a really strange wind: short, strong gusts followed by nothing, just absolute quiet.

The wind, more than anything else, accentuated the uncanny feeling around the campsite, and it took a long time before either of us fell asleep.

Day Forty-Two
Friday 29th April

Canning to Brookton to Mount Dale

The closer we came to the end of the Walk, the closer the distance between campsites. We had heard that this had been done intentionally to allow walkers to adjust to the Track, from the perspective that most people walk the Track from north to south. For us, having already walked so far, it was not so difficult to string together two campsites each day.

It dawned cold and overcast with a cool breeze blowing, and we left the shelter just after seven-thirty. The sensation of rain in the air was very strong, and it felt as though it could easily start raining at any moment.

The first kilometres provided fairly straight-forward walking through swampy flats. Although the ground was relatively dry when we did the Walk, I would imagine that at certain times of the year the whole area could easily turn into a quagmire. It was while we were walking this part of the Track that we met a group of walkers doing a four-day hike and, further along, two women walking on their own. Everyone was heading towards Sullivan Rock. The first group greeted us but did not stop, while the two women actually seemed grateful to be able to take a short rest, and they talked with us for the best part of five minutes. They were both very interested to hear that we had walked all the way from Albany, and they wanted to know what it had been like.

After eleven kilometres, we arrived at Brookton around ten o'clock in the morning, and we were delighted that we had managed to get so far without it actually raining. The section of the Track from Brookton Highway to the Brookton hut (about two and a half kilometres) has been built to accommodate people in wheelchairs. I did wonder just how easy it would be to navigate the entire distance in a wheelchair, but I dare say that it must be possible. The campsite itself is also built with disabled people in mind, which is a great idea. We took a short break, and enjoyed being able to lie completely prone just looking at the somewhat overcast sky. By eleven we were back on the Track and on our way to Mount Dale.

It was only 16°C, the cool breeze had not stopped blowing, and it was still overcast. We were, however, relieved that it was not raining.

The vegetation was now a mixture of jarrah, karri, marri, banksia, she-oaks and native grass; in other words, a combination of medium to tall trees and middle-range vegetation. There was also a good deal of low underbrush, which I assumed would be covered with flowers in the spring.

The walk was uneventful, and shortly after twelve we arrived at the Mount Dale campsite, which is surrounded by dense forest and situated at the base of a 546-metre-high mountain. The mountain (and later the campsite) had been named after Ensign Robert Dale, the first European to explore the area in 1829.

The Track, both north and south of the Mount Dale campsite, is not much more than soft sand, which does not make for particularly easy walking; however, that relatively small inconvenience paled in comparison with the campsite itself. Sadly, it was the dirtiest campsite we were to encounter on the Track (all, or most, of the campsites so far had been extremely well looked after by walkers).

Someone had left several very large plastic bags full of rubbish near the fireplace, and the bags, not particularly well closed, were completely covered with flies. Apart from, or perhaps because of, the rubbish, the whole campsite had an unpleasant, confined feeling about it, and had we not been expecting a fairly difficult day the following day we would almost certainly have pushed on. We tried to move our focus from the rubbish and, instead, attempted to appreciate the blue sky that was finally making a feeble, but concerted, attempt to push away all the grey.

It was still quite cool, and we sat in the shelter in our sleeping bags, our backs to the fireplace and what it contained, and read some old *Reader's Digests* that someone had left in the shelter. In spite of the rubbish and the flies, we were grateful for a rest afternoon as we had no idea what to expect the following day. We knew only too well that diversions could add kilometres to a day's walking.

We still had nothing more than a rumour of a realignment around the Beraking campsite (the campsite that had been burnt down in the December fires). We had tried to find out what was happening in the area, but our efforts had been in vain. When we first arrived at Mount

Dale, we thought that there might have been information in the shelter, but though we searched high and low there was nothing that gave any indication as to whether or not the realignment was likely to happen.

Day Forty-Three
Saturday 30th April

Mount Dale to Beraking to Waalegh

During the night, it finally rained, and for an hour or so the rain was quite heavy; then it stopped, only to start again at seven in the morning. As could be imagined, the rain did nothing to improve the campsite, but instead managed to emphasize all the disgusting rubbish and the horrible feeling of being closed in. I am fully aware that it was just our misfortune to end up at the campsite after a group of litterbugs, and that normally the campsite was probably no dirtier than any of the other sites; however, there was also something else about Mount Dale, something that was negative yet intangible and difficult to pinpoint. On reflection, this extra *something* could well have been nothing more than the combined impact of all the other negatives. Because we did not like the campsite, it was not at all difficult to leave it in the morning, and we were on our way well before eight o'clock, even though it was still raining lightly.

In spite of there having been no information in the Mount Dale shelter, we were still expecting some kind of diversion closer to Beraking, but we had no idea where that diversion was likely to start.

Fortunately, the rain soon eased off, and not long afterwards Jonathan noticed a timber stand which was minus its sign. Much later on we decided that the non-existent sign could well have been the sign indicating the beginning of the realignment, but as the sign itself was no longer there then someone must have removed it. Why on earth anyone would do such a thing was unfathomable. We wondered briefly if it was possibly the same person or persons who had left all their rubbish at the Mount Dale hut.

Consequently, we missed what was most possibly the diversion, and we continued along the original Track. After a while, we saw a Waugal pointing up a burnt and blackened hill and we followed it. However, it soon became very apparent that we were not on the Track: there were no more Waugals and definitely no track. Fortunately, Jonathan had the GPS, and, with the GPS, the compass and the map, we were eventually able to find our way, across fairly rough ground, around the sides of hills and across desolate valleys, to what was most probably the actual Track, not the diversion.

The whole area, stretching as far as we could see, was extremely sombre and black. There was not much green vegetation, though, in some places, clumps of burnt native grass had begun to send up new green spikes, and some of the trees already had spring-green leaves sprouting from black branches. It was, however, the blackened trunks and branches that stood out; black trees covered with thick black-grey soot.

We walked on, passing yet another burnt-out pine plantation and, almost by accident, discovered one of the

Track diversion signs. This sign led to another sign and another... and we followed them optimistically for quite some time. But eventually we reached a rather ambiguous point where we had the choice of turning to the left or continuing further up the hill. After some discussion, we chose the first alternative, which, as we later realized, turned out to be the original Track and not the diversion.

The further we walked, the more obvious it became that we were actually walking through the area that had been restricted. For a brief moment, we did consider backtracking, but by that stage we had already walked a considerable distance, and, given all the problems we had been having with signs, there was nothing saying that if we were to backtrack we would actually find the diversion.

Many of the trees looked as though they could easily fall down at the slightest provocation, and in some places, the ground underfoot occasionally gave way without warning to reveal large, gaping holes; at one point Jonathan almost fell into one of these hidden holes, and it was only some rather deft footwork that saved him at the very last moment.

The whole area was completely quiet and still, almost unearthly. There were no birds or animals, just blackened trees, soot-covered ground and complete and utter silence.

It was the silence that was the most desolating. Normally, when we say that a place is quiet, there are always lots of small non-essential sounds: sounds that are so much part of the background that we no longer really relate to them as sounds. Here, in this burnt-out forest, there were no non-essential sounds; there were no background sounds of any kind. It *was* completely and absolutely quiet.

We finally reached the devastated Beraking campsite around eleven-thirty. The blackened, destroyed building and campsite in the middle of all the sooty black forest was extremely moving, more so because of the complete isolation and the stillness. As we stood there, looking at the buckled sheets of iron and the remnants of what used to be a campsite, it was like being the only mourners at a funeral.

It felt as though we were intruding on something private, and we only stayed long enough to have a short rest and then we were on our way again.

The campsite at Beraking

All day we walked through soot-covered, scorched

forest, but, eventually, we reached the campsite at Waalegh, on the side of a mountain. It was just after two in the afternoon, and we could see where the fire had come right up to the campsite and had then suddenly stopped. It was a beautiful campsite and, after our disappointment with Mount Dale and a day of ravaged forest, we were extremely happy to be there.

Shortly after we had arrived and established ourselves in the shelter, it began to rain again. Sitting on the timber floor with a reliable roof over our heads, it was extremely pleasant to be able to look out on the rain without actually coming in contact with it. While we were admiring the absolutely fantastic view over the valley beyond the shelter, some emus wandered into the campsite area. They did not seem to be aware of our being there, but then a man, who we later learnt was called Roland, appeared from between the trees, and the emus very quickly disappeared.

Roland was the only person we had laid eyes on all day. He told us that he had done the whole Walk a few years previously and that he was now doing just a few days walking. As he talked, it became apparent that he had come from the direction of Mount Dale, exactly the same way as we had, so it was obvious that the diversion signs were not working. In his case, it was a bit more serious as he had not heard that Beraking had burnt down, and he had initially been expecting to spend the night there. Fortunately, it was not overly hot, otherwise he could have found himself without sufficient water.

During the night it literally teemed, making the three of us very thankful that we were actually in the shelter and not somewhere out on the Track. For some reason there were blinds on the open side of this particular shelter, which did help to retain a small amount of warmth.

Day Forty-Four
Sunday 1st May

Waalegh to Helena to Ball Creek to Hewett's Hill

We really did not intend to *triple up*, at least, not to begin with.

It was still raining when we got up, but then the rain stopped and the sun came out, and we were treated to an absolutely glorious morning. Thousands upon thousands of small water droplets, hanging from trees and bushes, glistened as the sun reclaimed its space and the last white and grey clouds disappeared from the sky.

We had left the shelter by seven-thirty but missed the Track diversion sign: there was a diversion on the northern side of Waalegh as well as on the southern side, owing to the same fire. We finally managed to find the realignment, then shortly afterwards we must have missed a second sign because we were no longer on the realignment and definitely not on the Track. Thanks again to the GPS, the compass and Jonathan's understanding of both, we were able to wend our way through a number of green pine plantations, and eventually reached the Helena River. When we first saw the river appear through the pine trees, we feared that we would have to reverse our steps, but the river was running low, and we managed to cross without getting too wet. Not long after crossing the river, we finally reconnected with the Track.

In spite of our very round-about walk from Waalegh to Helena, we arrived at the campsite before ten. We stayed for half an hour, and then we pushed on to Ball Creek.

Thankfully, the beautiful weather looked as though it had decided to stay, and the walking was not too difficult, even though the stretch between Helena and Ball Creek was reasonably hilly. In the main, the vegetation was wandoo, though there was also a lot of jarrah and yarri.

When we were almost halfway to Ball Creek, we saw the first person we had seen all day since leaving Roland at Waalegh. He was a Spaniard, and he told us that it was his second day on the Track. Like us, he was hoping to complete an end-to-end Walk, and he was aiming for Albany. He seemed particularly jovial and optimistic, and I remember that he had a toy monkey strapped securely to the back of his pack.

Mann's Gully, between Helena and Ball Creek, offered no problem from a descent/ascent point of view, but the whole place was filled with thousands of ferocious ants, every single one of them intent on devouring us alive. They were extremely focused and were definitely the cause of our ascending much faster than we descended.

We arrived at Ball Creek at twelve-thirty to find two men finishing their lunch. They acknowledged us but did not say much, then, as they were leaving, they came across to where we were sitting and wished us both all the best.

I changed socks, had a quick wash, and we were on our way just after one, having made the decision to triple up and do the next eleven-kilometre stretch to Hewitt's Hill.

The hills continued all the way to Mundaring Weir, which we reached shortly after two in the afternoon. The weir was constructed in the late 1890s and the lake created was initially called the Helena River Reservoir; later it became known as Lake C.Y. O'Connor. Charles Yelverton O'Connor was the Irish engineer who was responsible for the Goldfields Water Supply Scheme. This scheme allowed water from the Helena River Reservoir to be pumped for more than five hundred kilometres to the Mount Charlotte Reservoir in Kalgoorlie, the heart of the Western Australian goldfields. Politics and greed resulted in many slanderous comments concerning O'Connor, who, because of the nature of the project, was responsible for a very large amount of money. In 1902, O'Connor, unable to cope with the accusations, committed suicide by riding a horse into the ocean outside Fremantle and shooting himself. He left behind a wife and seven children. The scheme, which eventually proved to be of significant importance to the entire Western Australian economy, was finally opened the year after his death.

The weir being a tourist attraction and the day being a Sunday meant that there were *lots* of people everywhere, which was quite daunting. However, ignoring the crowds as much as it was possible, we found a small, out-of-the-way café, where we treated ourselves to salad, bread, mud cake, milkshakes and coffee, enjoying the ambiance of the open-fronted café, the nice food, the beautiful weather and the fantastic views across the weir.

We left around three, still with five or six kilometres remaining to Hewitt's Hill, and crossed the weir to the other side. From there, the Track continued on its rather hilly path towards the campsite, and as it twisted and turned we were treated to many great views over the weir.

We did not arrive at Hewitt's Hill until five, by which time the light was beginning to fade. We were both extremely tired after our thirty-kilometre day and were looking forward to nothing more than something to eat and our sleeping bags.

Also, we were both feeling a little sad, realizing that this would be our very last dinner on the Track, and I was silently wondering whether I would manage to return to any form of normality after six weeks of absolute freedom and solitude. Part of me wanted to continue as we had been – if only it had been possible – while another part was eager to move on to other things. There were so many new projects that I had thought up while walking, and I was excited about getting started.

While dinner was cooking, I caught up on my notes, and Jonathan lit some mosquito coils to deter the rather persistent mosquitoes. Then, almost as though it knew that it was the end of the road, my pen died.

We had just started eating, and the darkness had well and truly settled over the campsite, when we heard ominous rumblings. Before we had a chance to get our minds around the possibility of a storm, the sky lit up with an explosive display of lightning flashes, and almost immediately sheets of heavy rain obscured everything that was more than a metre beyond the shelter. Although there had been much rain on the Track, this was our first thunderstorm.

The pen might have died, but the rain had no such intention; it was torrential and it was incessant. Being outside in an open shelter during such a storm was quite frightening, the lightning and thunder seeming ever so much closer, and I found it extremely difficult to fall asleep.

Day Forty-Five
Monday 2nd May

Hewett's Hill - Kalamunda

This was our very last day on the Track. It was difficult to comprehend that it was the end: walking every day had become not only a well-entrenched routine but also a way of life. We had been walking for more than six weeks, and we had had an absolutely marvellous time in spite of blistered feet, heavy packs and the not infrequent feeling of being somewhat inadequate to the challenge ahead. I really did not want it to end; if it had been possible to rewind the entire six weeks I would have done so. I remember hearing about one man who got to the end of the Walk and then turned around and walked back another one thousand kilometres. For him the Walk had definitely become a way of life. In so many ways, our Walk had been all we could have hoped for and much, much more; indeed, it had been ever so much more satisfying and amazing than we had ever been able to anticipate.

It rained early, but by eight-thirty the rain had stopped and the sun had, thankfully, returned. Knowing that we had only ten kilometres ahead of us, we had a leisurely breakfast (for a change) and were ready to leave the shelter just before nine. I put the cover on my pack, just in case; however, it looked as though the day would be very much like the day before, sunny and warm.

Although it was somewhat hilly, the walking was relatively easy. We saw lots of wallabies, and then we passed the Calamunnda Camel Farm (a tourist attraction), and had glimpses of some of the camels. After we had been walking for about an hour, we noticed that the sky was getting much darker, and we made a unanimous decision to skip the break that we had been looking forward to. According to the map, we were fairly close to Kalamunda, and keeping our fingers crossed we continued to hope that we would arrive there before the rain came tumbling down again. However, we had not calculated with the very steep descent to the Brook and the equally steep ascent from the Brook on the other side.

The Track here was absolutely *awful*. There is no other word for it. There were lots of small, very loose rocks and hundreds of thousands of millipedes. Wherever we put a hand or a foot, thousands of the curious, investigative small creatures were immediately in just that very place, and were quickly crawling all over us. There were also just as many of the abominable gumnuts, and we decided that our situation was dire to say the least.

We went down and then up and then down, and then, in spite of all our hoping and praying, it *did* start to rain, and we were not really in a place or situation where we could have easily changed into wet-weather gear – we just prayed that the rain would not amount to anything serious, and we kept pushing on. Negotiating the final steep ascent from the Brook was a nightmare, as the rain by this stage was just as torrential as the night before, and the Track had turned into a major creek. There was nowhere to walk but in the 'creek', and without any kind of wet-weather protection we were both sopping wet.

We missed a Waugal and continued much further along the track than we should have. After trudging through some very difficult patches – slippery, clayey, gumnut-strewn – we realized what we had done, and we had to retrace our steps through the same very slippery, difficult area. Finally, we found the turnoff that we had missed and started on the very last bit of the Track.

It was still raining, but we were completely saturated by this stage, so it really did not matter any longer; all we could think about was reaching the Northern Terminus. We had assumed all along that the Northern Terminus would be much the same as the Southern Terminus and that there would be a dry, cosy building with happy, positive people to greet us (and, perhaps, the possibility of changing out of wet clothes). As it turned out, such was not the case at all.

The Northern Terminus was no more than a sign stating that we had reached the Northern Terminus. There was no little house, no one to greet us with a welcoming smile, no registration book. Nothing.

We took photos of each other standing near the sign in the teeming rain, and then we looked around for somewhere where we could possibly get out of the rain and, hopefully, change.

Beyond the sign, the bush quickly came to an end; in

front of us was Railway Road, and, on the other side of the road, a conglomeration of buildings that had all the markings of a shopping centre. Whether it was the time of day, the weather or a combination of both, Kalamunda seemed to be fairly deserted, which probably was just as well.

We crossed the road to the shopping centre and squelched through its shiny glass and tiled interior to the toilet section, causing a few raised eyebrows. Fortunately, the toilet area was quite decent. Jonathan looked after the packs while I went and changed and then I did the same for him.

It felt wonderful to be dry once more. While we were standing there deciding on our next move, a kindly cleaner came over and talked to us. She thought that the Walk sounded as though it must have been lots of fun; however, she could not understand why we would now be planning to spend a few days in Perth; she was very explicit that we should go to Melbourne instead. She had recently spent a few days in Melbourne, and Melbourne was *definitely* the place to go. If we did not want to go to Melbourne then we should at least go to Fremantle, but not Perth – according to the cleaner, there was absolutely nothing to do in Perth. She graciously showed us how to get to the bus station, reminding us, yet again, to reconsider spending time in Perth. We assured her that we would think about what she had told us and hurried to the bus stop, where, fortunately for us, there was a bus waiting.

It felt very strange to be sitting on a bus, surrounded by other people, because a large part of me was still somewhere out on the Track. From the windows of the bus we could see that Kalamunda (two Noongar words meaning *home* and *forest*) is a nice place with lots of leafy gardens; however, although we were aware of the streets and houses moving swiftly past the windows of the bus, we were content to sit back and do nothing. We had actually achieved what we had set out to do: we had walked one thousand kilometres. It was an awesome realization.

In Perth, we got off the bus at William Street and, after crossing the bridge over the railway lines, we soon reached the youth hostel, where, not having booked anything in advance, we felt that we were very lucky to get two quiet rooms. We washed a few clothes, showered, phoned home to let everyone know that we had actually arrived, and an hour or so later found an Indian restaurant nearby where we had a celebratory dinner. We were back at the hostel by ten-thirty and went to bed, still trying to get our minds around the fact that we had done what we had said we would do and that we had walked all the way from Albany to Perth.

Afterword

It felt very strange getting out of bed the following morning, Tuesday 3rd May, knowing that there was no need to walk anywhere that day. Jonathan was planning to do some work, having been able to borrow the computer at the youth hostel, and, with the weather showing a marked improvement on the previous day, I decided to go for a short walk, even if it was actually not necessary.

When I got back after about an hour, we had breakfast and then walked to the Bibbulmun Track Foundation office on Hay Street (not quite two kilometres) to register as having finished the Walk. There we met Gwen, the lovely lady who had been so helpful when I was planning the Walk, and spent some time talking with her. In fact, we were there for the best part of two hours.

Over the following days, we did many of the things that tourists do. We took the ferry to Fremantle, as the cleaner in Kalamunda had suggested we should, and we were suitably impressed. Perhaps because of all the beautifully preserved buildings from the 1800s, Fremantle has a definite European feel about it, especially the part closest to the harbour. We spent the whole day there; then, after watching the sun set in the west over the ocean, a sight that is completely impossible on the east coast of the continent, we caught the evening train back to Perth.

We visited art galleries, walked through Kings Park, visited The Bell Tower (with its eighteen bells, twelve of them donated by St Martin-in-the-Fields) and took a lift to the thirty-third floor of St Martin's Tower, where we drank coffee in a revolving restaurant while looking out over the man-made environment of the city below us.

Finally, on Saturday 7th May, while still enjoying beautiful, sunny weather, we packed up our things for the very last time, before calling a taxi to the airport, the first stage of our long trip home.

ΘΘΘΘΘΘ

I do not believe that we were *exactly* the same two people who returned to the east coast: six weeks and one thousand kilometres had wrought many changes in us, some subtle, some less so. Change is part of life, and every change, either for the better or the worse, must always impact on who we are and where we are going. All the changes brought about by our Walk were positive in their own way; we could see everyday situations from many new perspectives, and we had had lots of time to think about all those things that the pace and stress of living tend to push to one side.

A 1,000-kilometre Walk is undoubtedly a fairly drastic weight-loss method and possibly not one that is likely to gain widespread favour; neither of us set out to lose weight, but we both reached Perth many kilos lighter than when we left Albany. Losing weight was simply one of the side effects, like the almost obsessive need to keep walking. Even after we had returned home, I found it very difficult to break the habit of walking everywhere, and on my way to work of a morning I would get off the bus halfway to the railway station and walk the remaining three or four kilometres.

Two months after finishing the Walk, I handed in my resignation at work. I loved my job: it was stimulating and extremely satisfying, and I had been there for sixteen years, but I now knew that there were other things that I needed to do, and life is not eternal, even if we would like it to be. I involved myself in all those *other things*, and Jonathan moved overseas for a couple of years.

Although change, choice and challenge might well be regarded as important parts of the scaffolding to which life clings, we do not always have complete control over all of the changes and challenges; we do, however, usually have control over our choices. By exercising our freedom to occasionally choose specific challenges and to instigate positive changes in our lives, we are able to climb just that little bit higher up the scaffolding or move just that little bit further to either the right or the left. In both cases, we will certainly experience new perspectives and new opportunities.

Since Jonathan and I did the Bibbulmun Track, we have done many other Walks, both with each other and with others, but, because of its length and its intensity, the Bibbulmun Track still remains the most fantastic Walk we have done to date.

Acknowledgements

I am indebted to Monica, for her very patient and observant proofreading of the manuscript, and to Annette, for the wonderful cover design. I am also grateful to Andris for allowing me to use some of his photos from the Walk. Finally, my unreserved thanks go to Jonathan, not only for his support and encouragement during the Walk but also because without his participation it never would have eventuated.

A Note on Additional Sources

The book is about Jonathan's and my experiences on the Bibbulmun Track. For extra information – especially mapping information used in the track diagrams – I am grateful to *A Guide to the Bibbulmun Track* (Books 1&2), Department of Conservation and Land Management, 2nd Edition 2002, as well as the six Bibbulmun Track maps, Department of Conservation and Land Management, 1997[6].

---

[6] For guidebook information and updates refer to the Bibbulmun website https://www.bibbulmuntrack.org.au

DISTANCES BETWEEN CAMPSITES

FROM	TO	KMS
*Albany**	Hidden Valley	19.3
Hidden Valley	Torbay	17.5
Torbay	West Cape Howe	16.4
West Cape Howe	Nullaki	16.5
Nullaki	*Denmark*	16.4
Denmark	William Bay	15.1
William Bay	Boat Harbour	19.9
Boat Harbour	Peaceful Bay	22.7
Peaceful Bay	Rame Head	10.5
Rame Head	Giants	15.6
Giants	Frankland	13.7
Frankland	*Walpole*	17.5
Walpole	Mount Clare	10.0
Mount Clare	Long Point	12.2
Long Point	Woolbales	17.2
Woolbales	Mount Chance	20.4
Mount Chance	Dog Pool	19.4
Dog Pool	Maringup	24.5

Maringup	Gardner	15.9
Gardner	*Northcliffe*	15.1
Northcliffe	Schafer	14.0
Schafer	Warren	21.1
Warren	*Pemberton*	21.7
Pemberton	Beedelup	23.7
Beedelup	Beavis	19.5
Beavis	Boarding House	19.1
Boarding House	Tom Road	22.8
Tom Road	*Donnelly River*	15.9
Donnelly River	Gregory Brook	20.5
Gregory Brook	Blackwood	18.0
Blackwood	*Balingup*	17.7
Balingup	Grimwade	22.4
Grimwade	Noggerup	21.9
Noggerup	Yabberup	17.7
Yabberup	*Collie*	19.6
Collie	Harris Dam	21.3
Harris Dam	Yourdamung	13.6
Yourdamung	Possum Springs	18.6

Possum Springs	Dookanelly	19.3
Dookanelly	Murray	17.7
Murray	Swamp Oak	18.5
Swamp Oak	*Dwellingup*	13.1
Dwellingup	Chadoora	19.4
Chadoora	Mount Wells	14.9
Mount Wells	White Horse Hills	14.5
White Horse Hills	Gringer Creek	16.6
Gringer Creek	Nerang	16.6
Nerang	Mount Cooke	12.6
Mount Cooke	Monadnocks	12.7
Monadnocks	Canning	15.6
Canning	Brookton	11.1
Brookton	Mount Dale	8.3
Mount Dale	Beraking	11.5
Beraking	Waalegh	8.5
Waalegh	Helena	9.5
Helena	Ball Creek	8.6
Ball Creek	Hewett's Hill	10.6
Hewett's Hill	***Kalamunda***	10.2

www.ingramcontent.com/pod-product-compliance
Lightning Source LLC
Chambersburg PA
CBHW020107020526
44112CB00033B/1074